Paul Durcan was born in Dublin in 1944 [...]
He studied archaeology and mediev [...]
College Cork. In 1974 he won the Patrick Kavanagh Award and received Creative Writing Bursaries from The Arts Council/An Chomhairle Ealaíon, Ireland, in 1976 and 1980. He has given readings of his poems throughout the world. In 1981 he represented Ireland at the Struga Poetry Festival in Yugoslavia and in 1983, 1985 and 1986 undertook tours of the Soviet Union. In May 1985 he was resident poet at The Frost Place, New Hampshire. In February 1987 he gave readings in Saskatoon and Toronto, and in June 1987 represented Ireland at the Poetry International in Rotterdam. In March 1988 he gave readings in Montreal, New Brunswick and Nova Scotia, and in April 1988 undertook a tour of Italy. In June 1988 he read at the South Bank Festival of Poetry and in November 1988 gave readings in Paris, Luxembourg and Brussels. In February 1989 he returned to Canada to give readings in Toronto, New Brunswick and Newfoundland. In April 1989 he read at the Irish Festival in Leicester and in September 1989 at the Ilkley Festival. In October 1989 he received the Irish American Cultural Institute Poetry Award. In April 1990 he participated with the Estonian poet Jaan Kaplinski in the East European Forum at the ICA in London. In May 1990 he gave readings in Boston and New York. He is the 1990 Writer in Residence at Trinity College Dublin. He is a member of Aosdána.

Among Paul Durcan's published works are:

Endsville (with Brian Lynch), New Writers Press, Dublin, 1967

O Westport in the Light of Asia Minor, Anna Livia Press, Dublin, 1975

Teresa's Bar, Gallery Press, Dublin, 1976, 1986

Sam's Cross, Profile Press, Dublin, 1978

Jesus, Break His Fall, Raven Arts Press, Dublin, 1980

Ark of the North, Raven Arts Press, Dublin, 1982

The Selected Paul Durcan, Blackstaff Press, Belfast, 1982 (Poetry Ireland Choice), 1985

Jumping the Train Tracks with Angela, Raven Arts Press, Dublin/ Carcanet New Press, Manchester, 1983

The Berlin Wall Café, Blackstaff Press, Belfast, 1985 (Poetry Book Society Choice)

Going Home to Russia, Blackstaff Press, Belfast, 1987

In the Land of Punt (with Gene Lambert), Clashganna Mills Press, Dublin, 1988

Jesus and Angela, Blackstaff Press, Belfast, 1988

Daddy, Daddy

PAUL DURCAN

THE
BLACKSTAFF
PRESS

BELFAST

First published in July 1990 by
The Blackstaff Press Limited
3 Galway Park, Dundonald, Belfast BT16 0AN, Northern Ireland
with the assistance of
The Arts Council of Northern Ireland

Reprinted October 1990, November 1990, January 1991

© Paul Durcan, 1990
All rights reserved

Typeset by Textflow Services Limited

Printed by The Guernsey Press Company Limited, Guernsey, C.I.

British Library Cataloguing in Publication Data
Durcan, Paul, *1944*—
Daddy, daddy.
I. Title
821.914

ISBN 0-85640-446-2

ACKNOWLEDGEMENTS

Alpha; *Fortnight*; the *Irish Review*; *Making Sense*; *Stet*; the *Sunday Tribune*.

'Nights in the Gardens of Clare' is the text of an oratorio by Mícheál Ó Súilleabháin performed at the Ennis Arts Festival, 1988, by the Harmony Row Choir: Eamonn Cotter (flute); Gerard Grennell (flamenco guitar); Mícheál Ó Súilleabháin (synthesiser); Paul Durcan; and Lourda McKeown. Produced for RTE Radio 1 by Julian Vignoles, it received a Pater Award from the Australasian Academy of Broadcast Arts and Sciences.

'Amnesty' was read at the General Humbert Summer School in Castlebar, County Mayo, in August 1989.

'Lord United Ireland' was read on *First Edition*, RTE 1, Christmas 1989.

'The Centre of the Universe' is part of the text of *The Paul Durcan Suite* by Bill Whelan, performed by the London Chamber Orchestra at the National Concert Hall, 5 December 1988.

First and last, the author wishes to record his gratitude to C.C.S.

He liked gazing at the world, doing nothing.

Simone de Beauvoir, *Adieux*

to the memory of
JOHN JAMES DURCAN
of Turlough, County Mayo
1907–1988

CONTENTS

PART
I

Paul

In the rush-hour traffic outside the centre-city church
I stood with my bicycle waiting for the lights to change –
A Raleigh bicycle with upright handlebars
That I had purchased for two pounds fifty pence in The Pearl –
When a priest in black soutane and white surplice
Materialised in the darkness of the porch.
He glided over to me:
'I am about to begin a funeral Mass but I have no mourners.
Would you be prepared to act as a mourner for me?'

As we paced up the aisle, the priest enlightened me:
'He was about the same age as yourself,
All we know about him is that his name was Paul.'

I knelt in the front pew,
The coffin on trestles alongside me,
Its flat abdomen next to my skull.
I felt as a mother must feel
All alone in the maternity ward
With her infant in the cot at the foot of the bed,
A feeling that everything is going to be all right
But that we are all aliens in the cupboard,
All coat hangers in the universe.

The priest – a seven-foot-tall, silver-haired peasant in his
    eighties –
Instructed me to put my bicycle in the hearse beside the
    coffin.
The two of us sat in front with the driver.
At a major traffic junction near the cemetery of Mount
    Prospect
We had to brake to avoid knocking down a small boy.
The car behind us bumped into our rear bumper,

3

Inducing the bicycle to bump against the coffin.
We saw a prominent politician in the back seat blessing
   herself.
At the graveside as the priest said prayers
I got the feeling that the coffin was empty;
That Paul, whoever he was,
Was somewhere else.

'How do you know that his name was Paul?'
I asked the priest as we tiptoed away.
He handed me a creased sheet
Of blue vellum unlined notepaper – Belvedere Bond:
Dear Paul – Thank you for your marriage proposal
But I am engaged to be married in Rome in June.
Best wishes always, Mary

Queen of Loneliness.

The Half-Moon Blackbird

We are holding hands after four years
Of walking up and down the wall to the Half-Moon.
We bleed to believe in the beacons and the buoys.
We bleed to stand still in one another's shoes,
For what is affection but a shoe shop
In which to try on one another's shoes?
Just as we did in Palermo long ago
When we first met and you were shoeless
And you put on my sandals to get you home
Past the knives to the Hotel Presidente.
I hold your boot to my lips, its pigskin toecap.

William Lithgow in his Painefull Peregrinations of 1632
Has Comments Upon Sicily – I tell you –
'... and the best Corall in the world
Is found here, beside Trapani;
Growing under the water greene and tender,
But when arising above, it becometh red and hard'.

I turn away from the black waters of Dublin Bay
To contemplate the gilded boughs of your face glow
Inside the green leaves of your eyes.
A westerly gust whips up,
It is 6.05.07 on October the sixteenth 1988.
Bending in my direction, leaning towards me,
You are felled
Inside a snowstorm of falling leaves.
We leave the wall, not
To speak to one another – not ever again.
We dwell in the same terrace – the same terrace of stars
Separated by night.

I am a small girl in Clontarf, Dublin 3,

With slight brain concussion.
In the secrecy of my bedroom, I take down from my mantelpiece
A snowstorm in a glass ball, and I shake it:
Snowstorm around a slight half-moon of coral,
Green and tender, red and hard.

Ho Chi Minh

My birthday today – one year to the day
She stopped speaking to me. Got a plane home this morning
To Dublin from Leeds–Bradford. On the hall floor
A packet addressed to me in her flamboyant majuscule.
Hand delivered. Franked with no stamp.
A small anthology of North Vietnamese Women's Pain
Purchased last week in Ho Chi Minh Airport
In Ho Chi Minh City. When she was a girl in New York City
She had posters of Ho Chi Minh
On the bedroom wall of her cold water pad in the Village.
I flick through its minuscule, indecipherable pages.
Each paragraph of pain accompanied by a miniature batik,
Small women combing out their long black manes
While behind them in scurrying silence
Their small men tend to them,
Bowls of water dragged into focus.

I drag out from under the stairs an unopened brand-new
    suitcase
Which she gave me last year as a birthday gift
The day she stopped speaking to me.
I drop the little green book down into the depths of the
    suitcase,
Down into its synthetic silk drawers, and close it,
Putting it away for another year
In the cupboard under the stairs, where the mice are.
Collectively things look like what they sound like.
Ho Chi Minh.

Margaret, Are You Grieving?

From the contours of the envelope
It is a greetings card
For my birthday and by the Canadian
Postage Stamp – the Common Loon –
I can tell it must be
From my daughter in Montreal,
Where she's got a job in the bar
Of the Marguerite Yourcenar Reading Club.

I am cheekbone-smug, beard-proud
That she should remember my birthday,
Much less send me a card.
It's one of those
Tall as a telephone booth
Birthday Cards
With three words
In black capitals:
JESUS LOVES YOU.

Sweet and thoughtful of her.
Inside it continues in italics:
Everyone Else Thinks You're An Asshole.

I remember her when she was two years old
Playing hide-and-seek with me
Behind telegraph poles in the snow,
Lodgepole pines
Adrift in the early morning snow.
How then at dawn she giggled as then at midnight she
    screeched
At the spider in the plug hole of the sink.

No one will ever know what it was like

To spend so much as one night alone
And fugitive, penniless and homeless,
In the snow in downtown Montreal.
No one will ever know what it was like
To have been my daughter
Or what it was like to have been my daughter's father.

Wrist warmers; headphones; earmuffs; study lamps;
Because tomorrow's headlines are today's inscriptions
Does not make them any the less the original
And indecipherable inscriptions that they are:
'Father Hopkins Accused Of Writing Poems To Little Girls';
He sleeps in her boat while she rows him home.
'Jesus Loves You – Everyone Else Thinks You're An Asshole';
He sleeps in her boat while she rows him home.

And she's singing a song because she's that kind of girl
Who in darkness on water sings to her father:
'Donnybrook Garage,' she sings, 'Donnybrook Garage.'
And he's singing a song because he's that kind of man
Who in darkness on water sings to his daughter:
'Anglesea Road,' he sings, 'Anglesea Road.'
He sleeps in her boat while she rows him home.

Phyllis Goldberg

Of all the women working in our office
Phyllis Goldberg is the quietest, most polite, most solicitous,
Most diligent, most discreet, most generous.
She'd been with us about twenty years when she went sick
And George Webb asked me to drop in on her on the way
   home.
An old lady in a walking frame answered the door
And motioned me upstairs with her eyebrows.
She was sitting up in bed naked
With a bottle of whiskey in one hand
And a half-pint tooth mug in the other.
Feeling incongruous, I enquired:
'Is there anything I can do for you?'
She gazed upon me with tears in her eyes,
Owls of tears:
'Make love to me,' she said,
In a tone at once passionate and dispassionate.
Since boyhood I had dreamed of being seduced
By a woman in her bedroom
– Is there a man who has not? –
Yet now it was the last thing I wanted to do
Or have done to me.
I felt more incongruous than usual as I undressed,
Unbuttoning my crisp pink shirt over thin, hairy, white legs.

After we had made love
– Angry flesh –
She fell asleep
And I sat up in bed with her head in my lap,
Patting her damp brown hair.
As I came down the staircase
I felt like a minor French count
In a nineteenth-century film

After having strangled his mistress,
Putting on his top hat and white kid gloves,
Twirling his ivory-knobbed cane.
Her mother watched from her walking frame
As I crossed the hall floor to the door.
When I opened the door I was afraid to look back
In case I should find the walking frame empty.
As I picked my steps through the snow
All I could hear was an empty walking frame.
I began to hurry through the snow
For fear that the walking frame
Would begin to run after me.
No one will ever believe me
That I did what I did
Because it seemed what I ought to do.

That night Phyllis Goldberg telephoned me,
The first and only time that she telephoned me in twenty years.
'Thank you for making love to me,' she said.
'Oh, not at all,' I said,
'Glad to be – '
She put down the phone
And I sat down behind my desk in the dark,
At my silent word processor, with its chin in its hands,
And I waited.
I knew that it was only a matter of time
Before the door would open of its own accord
And in the half-light from the hallway
I would see the shadow of the walking frame.
I would cry out for help but it would be too late.
The next day a card from Phyllis Goldberg would swoop
    through my letter box
With such a flutter that everybody in the cinema would behold
Its butterfly trajectory:
'Thank you for making love to me. Love. Phyllis Goldberg.'

The Christies Foxhunters Chase over Three Miles and Two Furlongs

to Síabhra

I feel all saliva and go,
Applying my lipstick before the big race.
If I am going to fall,
I ask myself at which jump I will fall.
Will it be at the third ditch
Or at the second-last from home?
I anticipate the stony, mossy tones of the race commentator:
'Lonely Moorland has unseated his rider at the first.'

I purse my lips and swivel my tongue.
Betimes in dreams I find myself
Putting my tongue in my stirrup.
I extend my tongue to achieve maximum moisture.
It is a pale pink lipstick which I favour.
I check my bit.
If I were a man, I'd envy myself.
I smack my lips to seal my fate.
I feel in love with myself, which is a good omen.
Self-love is the secret of love.
If I love myself, I will love you.
Win or fall
I will have given all.

Felicity in Turin

We met in the Valentino in Turin
And travelled down through Italy by train,
Sleeping together.
I do not mean having sex.
I mean sleeping together.
Of which sexuality is,
And is not, a part.
It is this sleeping together
That is sacred to me.
This yawning together.
You can have sex with anyone
But with whom can you sleep?

I hate you
Because having slept with me
You left me.

The Centre of the Universe

I

Pushing my trolley about in the supermarket,
I am the centre of the universe;
Up and down the aisles of beans and juices,
I am the centre of the universe;
It does not matter that I live alone;
It does not matter that I am a jilted lover;
It does not matter that I am a misfit in my job;
I am the centre of the universe.

But I'm always here, if you want me –
For I am the centre of the universe.

II

I enjoy being the centre of the universe.
It is not easy being the centre of the universe
But I enjoy it.
I take pleasure in,
I delight in,
Being the centre of the universe.
At six o'clock a.m. this morning I had a phone call;
It was from a friend, a man in Los Angeles:
'Paul, I don't know what time it is in Dublin
But I simply had to call you:
I cannot stand LA so I thought I'd call you.'
I calmed him down as best I could.

I'm always here, if you want me –
For I am the centre of the universe.

III

I had barely put the phone down when it rang again,

This time from a friend in São Paulo in Brazil:
'Paul – do you know what is the population of São Paulo?
I will tell you: it is twelve million skulls.
Twelve million pairs of feet in the one footbath.
Twelve million pairs of eyes in the one fishbowl.
It is unspeakable, I tell you, unspeakable.'
I calmed him down.

I'm always here, if you want me –
For I am the centre of the universe.

IV

But then when the phone rang a third time and it was not yet
    6.30 a.m.,
The petals of my own hysteria began to wake up and unfurl.
This time it was a woman I know in New York City:
'Paul – New York City is a Cage',
And she began to cry a little bit over the phone,
To sob over the phone,
And from five thousand miles away I mopped up her tears,
I dabbed each tear from her cheek
With just a word or two or three from my calm voice.

I'm always here, if you want me –
For I am the centre of the universe.

V

But now tonight it is myself;
Sitting at my aluminium double-glazed window in Dublin
    city;
Crying just a little bit into my black tee shirt.
If only there was just one human being out there
With whom I could make a home? Share a home?
Just one creature out there in the night –

Is there not just one creature out there in the night?
In Helsinki, perhaps? Or in Reykjavik?
Or in Chapelizod? Or in Malahide?
So you see, I have to calm myself down also
If I am to remain the centre of the universe;
It's by no means an exclusively self-centred automatic thing
Being the centre of the universe.

I'm always here, if you want me –
For I am the centre of the universe.

Self-Portrait, Nude with Steering Wheel

I am 45 and do not
Know how to drive a car
– And you tell me I am cultured.

45 years creeping and crawling about the earth,
Going up and down the world,
And I do not know the difference between a carburettor and a
    gasket
– And you tell me I am a Homo sapiens.

45 years sitting in the back seat giving directions
– And you say that I am not an egotist.

45 years sitting in the passenger seat
With my hands folded primly in my lap
– And you think I am liberated.

45 years getting in and out of cars
And I do not know where the dipstick is
– And you tell me that I am a superb lover.

45 years of grovelling behind a windscreen
– And you talk of my pride and courage and self-reliance.

45 years of not knowing the meaning of words
Like transmission, clutch, choke, battery, leads
– And you say that I am articulate.

45 years of hovering on street kerbs and clinging to lamp
    posts
Terrified to cross the street
– And you whisper into my ear in the middle of the night that I
    am a Divine creature.

45 years bumming lifts off other people
– And you tell me I am an independent, solitary, romantic
  spirit.

So it is that you find me tonight
Loitering here outside your front door
Having paid off a taxi in three ten-pound notes,
Nude, with a steering wheel in my hands.

A Vision of Democracy in the County of Meath

When I got up this morning, I went out
To look at the rain. I had planned
To spend the morning with my gun,
Thinking about the story of my life.
But I saw that it was raining
And I decided to go out and have a look at the rain.
What struck me about the rain was how lit up,
Illuminated and fluorescent it was,
A bright rain of democracy.
The sky was grey as sheep
And tumbling over itself on low legs
But the rain was wearing lights under its tights
And strip lighting in the stitching of its jackets.
I saw in the park in front of the house
A Singer sewing machine freshly painted black.
Its treadle was pumping up and down.
When the woman who was sitting at it saw me look at her
She looked up and shaking her head a little
She smiled and shook her head a little again and stated:
'I am just an ordinary democrat',
And when I looked as if
I was about to reach for a quiver of words
She repeated herself without emphasis:
'I am just an ordinary democrat –
Take me as I am or not at all.'
I began to walk across the park towards her,
Ready to hand in my gun, ready to vote,
Ready to vanish, ready to disappear,
Wanting only to be her servant in all things great and small.
I will take you as you are or not at all.

The Pine by the Sea

after Carlo Carrà

North of the forest there is a bog
That marches on the horizon.
Setting forth across the heather
All that is visible is a Scots pine,
Five feet in height, yet fully grown,
A solitary sail upon the ocean of the bog.
Mosses of maroon, wine, magnolia-white,
Bog cotton, willowherb, frachan,
Clouds figure-of-eighting on the rink,
A moody sun, a breeze,
Silence humming to itself
Until some thirty metres from the pine
My eye focuses on a pink clump
Swaying between the waves of heather.
I become aware that it is a human bottom
And that there is a second human bottom underneath,
A pair of human bottoms, and what they are conjuring
By their playing
– Their swaying –
Is that in all that expanse of solitude
Under a single solitary Scots pine
There is only one form of existential
Etiquette that is correct
And bottomless.
In a finite world
Of accident and old age
A pair of bottoms
Under a pine
Is a sign
Of immortal bottomlessness.

The Dream of Life

A woman waiting for her man
In Dowth of the slow-footed consonants
Draws down the sash window of her bedroom.
A pair of house martins – the last house martins of summer –
From mud huts under eaves
Alight on the precipice
Of the top ledge of the window frame,
Testing their propellers, whirring,
The voyage to Africa,
Hawks in the cliffs of Sicily
Avid for food for their hawk chicks.

PART
II

Putney Garage

to Brian Fallon

The morning after the poetry reading
At the Poetry Society in Earl's Court Square
I decided to go to a film in Leicester Square,
Having already that auburn October day
Changed my mind five times.
I would catch the 4.35 p.m. showing
Of *Au Revoir Les Enfants* in the Premiere.
I strolled along the north side of Piccadilly
But the closer I came to the cinema
The more I felt like going home to Brixton,
To Bill and Pippa, Ben and Sam and Jo,
In 64 Milton Road,
Pampas grass in the front garden,
Up the lane from Electric Avenue,
The child's playground that is London in October,
Its wild mildness, its puberty,
Kick of spentoutedness in my calf muscles.

I crossed over to the south side of Piccadilly,
Retraced my steps.
At the bus stop outside the Egyptian State Tourist Office
Francis Bacon was waiting for a bus;
Those ancient, glittering eyes on black steel rods
Socketed in their Sicilian pouches;
That teenager's ageing mouth
All cheek and tongue-in-cheek.

I fell into line.
We stood in silence,
He lounging against the corner of the bus shelter
In a lounge suit,

Hands in trench-coat pockets,
Belted trench coat flapping open loose, horny epaulettes,
Black polished shoes, one over t'other,
Idly alert,
Courtly corner boy.

Luckily I had not got with me my pocket Olympus camera.
Two number 19s passed,
Flocks of cabs.
I did not allow advertisements for the pyramids
And for a boy Pharaoh
To distract me from the nape of Bacon's neck,
The henna-dyed hairs, gelled, spiky,
Gilded in October evening sun.
The breeze lifted the hair on the crown of his skull,
The proud, soft, blown comb of the cock.

A number 14 bus sailed into view,
The Statue of Eros in its rear-view mirror.
He put out his hand,
His left hand – bare, ungloved.
He stepped up onto the platform.
But although he was first in the queue
He stood back to permit
A young Asian gentleman,
Lean, prematurely grey,
To cut inside him to the lower deck.
Then he, aged eighty years,
Swung up the staircase like a gibbon
In the Dublin zoo.

I stepped back out of the queue,
Mulling on Vincent's memorial in Auvers
By Osip Zadkine – man at work or
Study of a man in a landscape.

I studied him sit himself down
Halfway down the aisle of the upper deck
On the north side.
What to call it? And by whom?
'Good Evening, Childhood' by J. M. W. Turner?
The bus sailed out into the smog-scrapered sun
Towards Hyde Park and Kensington,
Its terminus in white on black:
Putney Garage.

Hommage à Cézanne

This morning when I am trying to get myself together for
    work,
Piece myself together for work,
Shaving with one hand and making coffee with the other,
There's a ring on the door bell and it's Olympia:
'There's a horse on my staircase, Paul.'
I am forty-three – Olympia is nineteen.
She stands there laconically
In a miniskirt the size of a hanky
And a black bowler hat and a white blouse
And a green suede hunting jacket:
'There's a horse on my staircase, Paul.'

I do not know what I am supposed to do about it.
I rock on the backs of my heels,
Trying to wipe the shaving cream from off my face
And glancing down at the span-new coffee stain
On my turquoise cotton shirt.
She gives me the sort of cat-on-the-wall smile
That twangs its garters between tail-swishes:
'You and I have a secret
But neither of us knows what it is.'

I do not know what it is.
Foggily, I do not know what it is.
Then she says that thing to me again:
'There's a horse on my staircase, Paul',
And just as I am about to say to her 'Come in',
She steps up to me on the tips of her toes
And flicks me a kiss high on the cheekbone
And spins around and steps back into the elevator.
I step back into my apartment
And squirt some shaving cream into my coffee filter

And stir my mug with my razor:
'There's a horse on my staircase, Paul.'

I am walking around in circles in my own apartment.
I am supposed to be at work one hour ago.
What am I supposed to say to my boss?
My boss is a chic fifty-seven-year-old mother-of-five:
'Paul, why don't you go to sleep for a week?
We can take a look at your equestrian needs
When you get to feeling a little less hysterical.'

Am I dreaming?
No, I am not dreaming.
I can hear the sound of my own hooves
Stamping on the marble steps of her staircase.
I go back to sleep again
To the sound of my own hooves
Stamping on the marble steps of her staircase:
'You are a horse on my staircase, Paul.'

Reading Primo Levi by the Family Fireside at Evening

I turn the pages, wisdom
Dissolving into despair.
When woman and child speak to me
I do not hear them.
What am I to do?
Continue the book,
Pursue the truth,
Make sad the family?

Or close the book
And into the hole in my head
Let lamplight filter?
Little Mark wants to know
If I will play Labyrinth.
Holding the book open in my hand,
I tell him that I can't
Play Labyrinth.
'Why can't you?' he enquires.
I put down the book on the floor
And repeat: 'I can't.'
'Why can't you?' he enquires,
And I say, 'I don't know',
And I stand up and I leave the living room
And I go downstairs into the kitchen
Where I can be alone
Beside the oven
With the dog and the cat,
Fódhla and *Ketchel*,
And press my two hands against the sides of my head,
Palms on temples,
To try and stop
This fallingdownbackwards from my chimney,
This callingbackupatme from my stairwell.

'Will you play a game of Labyrinth?'
I can't, I can't. You must, you must.

Loosestrife in Ballyferriter

to Brian Friel on his sixtieth birthday

Dear Master – Homesick for Athens
In this summer of rain, I prayed to the Mother
Of God but she did not appear to answer
And the Loosestrife in Ballyferriter near broke my heart.

But then I came to the Gallarus Oratory.
Its small black doorspace was a Mount of Venus.
Within the womb of that miniature iconostasis
What I saw was a haven white as salt.

An Trá Bhán, an Trá Bhán,
Cá bhfuil m'athair, cá bhfuil mo mháthair?
An Trá Bhán, an Trá Bhán,
Cá bhfuil m'athair, cá bhfuil mo mháthair?

I stood in a delivery ward outside the Gallarus Oratory,
Surprised by coachload after coachload of tourists
From Celtic, from Medieval, from Modern times,
Expiring, only to be given birth to, in that small black doorspace.

The embryonic majority were from the Heel of Italy.
There were French, Swedish, German, Dutch.
There were siblings also from North America
To whom Ireland is an odyssey odder than Iowa.

VI

('Iowa' – she keened from behind a drystone wall –
'Iowa – I don't want to have to go to Iowa.
Iowa doesn't want me and I don't want Iowa.
Why must I forsake Ireland for Iowa?')

VII

There was a traffic snarl-up at the Gallarus Oratory,
All of the newly born vying to find parking space
In a gauntlet of fuchsia. In the small black doorspace
I gave vent to my grief for my foreign mother.

VIII

What is the nature of Loosestrife in Ballyferriter?
What class of a massacre occurred on the Great Blasket?
Who burned the islanders out of their island homes?
Was it the Irish who burned us out of our island homes?

IX

What we did not know as we scurried out over the waves
In the rain-laden sunlight to feed our eyes on the corpse of the
    Blasket
Was that we were being observed from a small black
    doorspace
By a small old man darker than his own doorspace.

X

Only the small old man living alone in his own black
    doorspace,
Counting us swooping in and out of the corpse of the Blasket
In the showdown, saluted me and he whistled in the cosmos,
His eyes peering out of the sheep's carcass of his skull,

His larynx thinned by the white sand of his eyes:
'It was the Irish who burned us out of our island homes',
And his smile was moist so that it stuck on the breeze:
'It was the Irish who burned us out of our island homes.'

An Trá Bhán, an Trá Bhán,
Cá bhfuil m'athair, cá bhfuil mo mháthair?
An Trá Bhán, an Trá Bhán,
Cá bhfuil m'athair, cá bhfuil mo mháthair?

Dear Master – Homesick for Athens
In this summer of rain, my closest grief
Lies in Tyrone dust. There is no man
Who would not murder his brother. Joy of all who grieve.

There is no God – only his Mother;
There is no God – only his Mother and;
There is no God – only his Mother and Loosestrife;
There is no God – only his Mother and Loosestrife in
    Ballyferriter.

Seamus Heaney's Fiftieth Birthday

I am disconcerted by all this cant of your fiftieth birthday,
Yet here I am at your sill with my tray of images,
Finding as I had hoped and half expected
A 'Please Do Not Disturb' sign on the door knob.
I put it down on the floor, glimpsing through the keyhole
A mistle thrush's nest in the font of a roofless side chapel.
What are they gossiping about? What can they mean?
As if you were a kind of superannuated dropout
In some Tahiti of the mind
Being girded up about the frothy loins
With grass skirt and a straw hat
Or a Buddha on Broadway or an anointed gangster
With sceptre and orb in a TV studio.

Do they not yet know the stations of innocence?
That you have three ceremonies to attend to on your
    birthday?
At the first of which there is the liturgy of your real absence;
At the second of which there is the liturgy of your immortal
    oblivion;
At the third of which there is the liturgy of your sublime
    unimportance;
One candle;
Altar girl with blue jeans showing beneath red soutane
And altar boys in Doc Martens
Hug candle snuffers with shy pride,
The cook's own sons and daughter.

She stands alone in the kitchen, watching the light on the
    estuary,
Waiting on the oven and the tide,
A small woman elevated on the rim of the turning world;
A Vision of Ingredients in the Twentieth Century;

Royal Baking Powder, eggs and butter, sugar and flour;
The silence coming in, and the silence going out;
Promontory, ewe, lamb; chapel, stone wall, water.
Her cookery encyclopaedia is open on a missal stand;
The poinsettia on the windowsill is chanting;
And the cat among the cruets is asleep.
Fie on your fiftieth birthday! What blasphemy!
I wish you well, married priest of the night stair,
You who, without cant, in our time
Redeemed the noun 'oven' from the rubric of murder
And gave back to us a verb of our mother:
To mother and to mother and to mother –
That one day we would feel warm enough to speak.

Tullamore Poetry Recital

It was a one-man show in Tullamore,
'The Sonnets of Shakespeare'.
The newspaper advertisement bubbled:
'Bring Your Own Knitting.'
The audience of twenty-five
Was devout, polite, attentive,
All with their knitting,
Men and women alike with their knitting.
I shut my eyes and glimpsed
Between the tidal breakers of iambic pentameter
The knitting needles flashing like the oars of Odysseus.

But as the evening wore on, and the centuries passed,
And the meditations, and the thanksgivings,
And darkness fell, and with it a fullish moon,
Not quite full but fullish,
Putting on weight by the teaspoonful,
One was aware of a reversal advancing,
Of incoming tides being dragged backwards.
The knitting needles were no longer oars
But fiddles in orchestras sawing to halts.
One became aware of one's own silence.
One was no longer where one thought one was.
One was alone in the pit of oneself, knitting needles.

The Barrie Cooke Show, May 1988

After the Barrie Cooke show,
Although I had no money,
I took a taxi back
To my room in Ringsend.

With no money in my pockets
I flew in a Mercedes Benz
Back to my room in Ringsend.
From the back seat of the taxi
- Blue Cabs No. 1379 –
I gave my blessing to the world,
To the left of me,
To the right of me.

After I'd borrowed the fare off a neighbour
And waved goodbye to the taxi driver
I stripped off my clothes.
I stretched out on my bed
And I opened my window –
My window with the broken sash
Propped up by a jar of Vaseline
Put there by the previous tenant,
A beautiful lady who died of cancer –
And I let in the wind and the sun
And I switched on the telly
And I watched the end of a one-day
County cricket match in Essex:
Seven runs to win
And five balls to bowl.

Naked I lay face down on my bed
With my head propped up in my left hand
While I looked back over my right shoulder at the telly.

My legs were spread-eagled on the duvet
And I could feel the breeze at the base of my spine
And on the root of my coccyx.
When you touched me there once with your forefinger
I stepped off a plane in midair.

Seven runs to win
And five balls to bowl.
When you touched me there once with your forefinger
I stepped off a plane in midair.

The Artist's Mother Visits Her Son's Sold-Out One-Man Exhibition

'I like his still life,
Its tone.
His self-portraits are not half bad.
But of course they are not a bit like him.
Actually he is awfully good-looking.
He has got beautiful hair, natural colour
Which does not show up in the portraits.
I like that one of himself standing at the end of the bed.
His slipover really looks like a slipover, doesn't it?
You can see it is made from wool, can't you?
I knitted it the Easter before last.
But I like his still life.
Another one of himself. I don't like him in that.
I know that smile.
It is so typical of him – having a plate on the floor.
He is always doing that. Putting his empty dinner plate
Down on the floor beside the leg of his chair.
Knife and fork neatly laid back down as always.
Are we ready for the off?
This is my first time seeing his pictures.
I cannot get into his studio, there are steps up to it.
I'd like to have one more look at his still life.'

Sucking in her jowls, she rests her hands on her wheel rims,
Staring up at a still life of a fish gleaming from a dish.

Heptonstall Graveyard, 22 October 1989

In Heptonstall graveyard,
Mid-ocean in Heptonstall graveyard,
I bob around Sylvia's grave,
My flag of hope unfurled.

I try to put away from me
Gossip and the Sunday newspapers.
I try to remember who you are.
I try to recollect the future.

Among sycamores I secrete myself
While another ancient mariner seeks Sylvia's grave.
He passes within an oar of me without seeing me.
Eighteen or nineteen, long curly red hair.

I resent his extreme youth, his extreme beauty.
I resent his cruising in Heptonstall graveyard.
I resent his trawling for Sylvia's grave.
I resent his discovery of Sylvia's grave.

He moors at the jetty of Sylvia's grave, smiling,
Tears climbing like worms out of his eyes.
He lays down a bouquet and rows off, rapidly;
Anchoring at the gate to blow kisses, formally.

I stroll back over to Sylvia's grave, smugly.
On the wrapping paper of a bouquet of Michaelmas daisies
There is a message scrawled in black Bic Biro.
It says: *Dear Sylvia, I Love You, Mike.*

I am put in my place.
You, and you, and you are put in your place;
His massive fierce-flamed penis between her tiny breasts,
Flowering between her golden lotuses.

Dairine Vanston, 1903–1988

to Sarah

I am driving a car belonging to a dead man
In the highlands of Costa Rica,
Thinking of the Howth tram.

My self-portrait has taken
Thirty-eight years to complete.

I have decided to complete it
And to die
And to throw my brassiere to the gulls
And to go dance on the roof of my father's home
Near the East Link Toll Bridge.

PART
III

The Death of the Ayatollah Khomeini

The day the Ayatollah Ruhollah Khomeini died
In a suburb in northern Teheran
I went to 12 noon Mass in Drogheda.
Although the temple was three-quarters empty,
The sixty-five-year-old, erect, creamy-haired pastor
Preached with passion.
He spoke deliberately, with precision and clarity;
With mercy, also, sense and charity.

'Young people of Drogheda' – he said –
'I beg you not to come to church on Sundays.
Sunday churchgoing has become a scandal.
You are young and open and sincere.
I beg you to remain young and open and sincere
To yourselves and to one another;
To live out the gospel on weekdays
In all its idealism.
On Sundays I beg you to stay in bed
While your parents get up to go to church.
We – the older generations –
Have become a nation of Sunday churchgoers.
The gospel means nothing to us on weekdays.
Our religion is comfort and the supermarket.
We have betrayed you.
Either we have given you bad example
Or we have given you no example.
We are insincere in word and in deed,
Most especially in word.
Not satisfied with having put doors on our emotions
Where there were no doors before,
We have closed the doors of our emotions.
Young people of Drogheda,
The roof of my church is unworthy of you.

Stay in bed on Sundays and dream
Of how life might be
When it is on earth as it is in heaven.'

The silence after he had spoken
Was the silence of a newly baked cake,
To be savoured by the actual sight of it,
Fresh out of oven.
As he approached the commemoration of the last supper
And the metamorphosis of bread and wine
Into body and blood
The congregation looked awake, alert, apprehensive,
As if we were in danger from the priest
Or as if he were in danger from us
Or as if we were all in danger together
As the moment of truth approached.
There was that sense of the moment of truth approaching.
There was an air of drama, expectation, butterflies.

As he began to annunciate the fatal, fateful words,
An infant girl in yellow smock,
Barely able to stagger,
Pink cardigan and white sandals,
Began to waddle up the centre aisle.
She did not know
Where she was going.
She was exploring
The far end of the garden,
Risking marbled, chrysanthemum borders.
She arrived at the steps of the altar
And gazed at the priest
High up above her.
The priest looked like a young naked woman
Looking down from a height
Upon a small, frock-coated, middle-aged gentleman.

'Do this in commemoration of me,'
He was saying and she nodded her head
And cried out, 'I will',
And turned around
And waddled all the way back down the aisle
Chanting
'I will'.
We all turned our heads to observe her.
She did not look back.
She left the church like a young bride never to return –
The young mother-to-be
Of the Ayatollah Ruhollah Khomeini.

The Sign of Peace

Being a middle-aged woman,
I do not often attend Mass
But when I do, the part I like
Is the bit where everybody is meant
To give one another the Sign of Peace.
The priest intones: 'In the name of Christ Jesus
Let us give one another the Sign of Peace.'

This morning when I found myself next
A bald small man with fiery eyes
I felt a spurt of something in my side
And when it came to the Sign of Peace
Without thinking about it
I turned around, as if in a trance,
And kissed him on both cheeks.

His eyes flapped their wings at me
And flew low across his cheeks
And he pushed out his two arms around me
And standing on tippy-toes
He kissed me one quick peck on the lips.
I could hear the gates of heaven clang open wide
And choirs of angels serenading us with raised spears.

You can imagine my surprise when at lunch time
I got a phone call from the parish priest to say
That the annual house-to-house parish collection
Was being made this afternoon
And that envelopes were to be returned not later than Wednesday
And that by the way, my dear child of God,
The Sign of Peace is never given in the form of a kiss.
The Sign of Peace is given always in the form of a handshake.

The cheek of him.

Mary Magdalene at Sunday Mass in Castlebar

With my head in my hands
I am draped across a pew,
The epitome of sanctimoniousness.
I look up and observe in profile
A middle-aged lady receiving Holy Communion
From the parish priest at the altar rail.
She is small, stout, stately,
Balanced on black high heels,
Red leather miniskirt,
Red leather jacket with gold buttons,
Black tights.
She sticks out her bubbly pink tongue.
When she carousels round to return
Back down the centre aisle
Her hands are pinnacled in prayer
Between the cleavage of her breasts,
Her violet varnished fingernails bejewelled
In translucent violet Rosary beads,
Violet purse under arm,
Face charred black with white powder,
And her red berry eyes – her pithy haws –
Are not closed but open, wide open,
Facing right down to the back of the church,
Looking the west door straight in the bull's eye,
Just as they were that Thursday night
At supper time in Jerusalem three months ago;
The young bull sitting up at the head of the table
Taking care, taking care of her.

Shanghai, June 1989

to Catherine Byron

Taking in the washing from the line,
I am replaying the six o'clock TV news.
'A bullet in the back of the head
Is the traditional Chinese method of execution' –
The newscaster is telling us
As we watch a blue-smocked student
Standing bowed between two guards
In the dock of a kangaroo court.
I come upon a pair
Of panties, canary-yellow,
With floral sprigs for decoration,
Frilliness,
Fearfully feminine,
Bloodstained.
The label says: Made In China,
67% Polyester, 33% Cotton.
A boy in blue smock
Manufactured these frilly panties.

My own Aunt Cleena worked all her life
In the Irish Cotton Sewing Company.
In darks of winter dawns and dusks
She bicycled to and from work
For forty years
After the revolution.
She was a tiny lady with a stutter,
Most fearfully feminine,
And she was a great lady
For the frilly panties
With floral sprigs for decoration,
For wearing smocks
And blue in everything –

50

Blue cloche hat with matching
Blue gloves and blue shoes.
Only her lipstick was not blue.
She was a great small lady
For reading banned books by Graham Greene
And Aldous Huxley
And going to two Masses every day,
Sometimes three,
And alluding to forbidden topics –
Evolution, ecumenism.
She was a great small lady
For conversing with strangers at bus stops,
Preferably small gentlemen
Of her own stature and greatness.
She died of loneliness
Getting in or out of bed.
Her carmine-painted lips turned blue
And she was bleeding
From the wainscoting of her tiny mouth.
A replica in miniature of her father's exit,
A bullet in the palate,
Executed in the name of politics.

I put back the panties on the line,
Take twelve paces back into the trees
And with my brother's shotgun
Fire a single bullet,
Blasting a hole
Through all that femininity,
All that canary-yellowness,
All that frilliness,
Bloodstained,
All that impurity of being female.
I pin them to the wall of the Irish parliament.
These are my daughter's panties.

Member of the European Parliament

It was Good Friday lunch time in the Canaries.
We were planning to attend the holy ceremonies at 4 p.m.
In the compound chapel in Puerto Rico.
I was sitting out on our balcony
Preening myself and reading biographies
Of Ernest Hemingway and Nora Barnacle.
I was reading the two of them
At the same time.
I was aware of the couple on the balcony below
Pottering about but I was so preoccupied
With Ernest Hemingway and Nora Barnacle
Changing places on my lap
That I was only aware of them.
It only dawned on me
That what they were doing
Was having intercourse
Underneath a table that had an enormous bowl
Of apricots perched on its edge.

I kept looking back down at my pair of biographies
For fear of catching myself out looking at the couple.
Although I am no paragon myself,
A bit of a gull in point of fact,
I found it difficult to believe my eyes.
I tried to pretend to myself
That I was not seeing what I was seeing.
What made it inconvenient
Was that I knew the couple,
Or rather, I knew him
And I knew that she was his research assistant in Brussels.
They were spending Holy Week in the Canaries
To refresh his Spanish.
In fact it was this couple

With whom we had arranged to attend
The Good Friday ceremonies.
While we stood in the bare stripped-down chapel,
About two hundred kilometres off north-west Africa,
With its stained-glass windows by Engels O'Hara,
Contemplating the details of the Crucifixion,
Two Irish couples,
My mind was on only one thing,
On one thing only,
The image of a member –
A purple-gummed hedgehog
Expanding –
Protracting and retracting
Underneath a table that had an enormous bowl
Of apricots perched on its edge.

Later in the wine bar, when the topic of conversation
Came round to the Holocaust, he got even more hedgehoggy,
Self-righteous and scornful, and he said to me:
'I have to say
That I am a Member of the European Parliament.'
'I know you are' – I answered him.

The Deep Supermarket, Next Door to Ajay's

Traipsing the streets of Leicester city
In need of refreshment, I went into a shop
Called The Deep Supermarket.
It had a low ceiling and it was long and narrow and dark
And crammed with produce.
Behind the till, barely visible, barely audible,
Stood a small Asian woman whose beauty
Was such that I found it awkward to look at her
Straight in the eye.
'May I have two apples?' I asked her.
'I am sorry' – she replied in a low voice –
'I do not have apples,
But if you try Ajay next door
I am sure he will be able to oblige you very well.'

Back out on the pavement
I glanced back up at her shop
And at its name, The Deep Supermarket,
And at the name of the shop next door,
Ajay's.
I went into Ajay's.
A small, lean, stout man with a moustache
Who stood at the till declared:
'Good Afternoon, Sir',
As if he had been waiting all afternoon
For my arrival and for the transaction
We were about to undertake and enact.

Ajay's shop, by contrast with The Deep Supermarket,
Appeared to have almost no stock,
Appeared to be almost empty,
Except for being provisioned with daylight from two sides,
Being situated, as it was, on a street corner.

There were a few shelves
With piles and arrays
Of rice and tea, and cardboard boxes
Of tins of curry powder, and trays of confectionery,
And on the floor, three or four cartons of fruit.
I picked up two shiny green apples and handed them to him.
He loaded them into the prewar weighing scales
Behind the prewar cash register.
Having meticulously calculated their weight,
He asked me for thirty-two pence.
He dropped the two apples into a brown paper bag
Which he twirled to fold
And as he handed it over to me he declared Thank You
With such rectitude, such solicitude,
That I felt as though it was I
Who had sold him the apples.
On an impulse of need as well as of etiquette
I considered a second purchase was in order.
'May I have a small bottle of Lucozade?'
He smiled gently – 'I am sorry, sir,
I do not have Lucozade
But if you go into The Deep Supermarket next door
I am sure she will be able to oblige you very well.'
As I took my leave of him
He said Goodbye
With such accentuated warmth
That I glanced back over my shoulder at him
And I saw in a sepia print of my dead father,
Hayseed in his hair,
A shy young man in a field in Mayo raking hay
Or in Sind.
I went back into The Deep Supermarket
And as Ajay had promised,
She stocked Lucozade in The Deep Supermarket.

She contemplated me curiously, sympathetically,
As I pocketed the change.

I continued traipsing on towards the outskirts of Leicester
In a caravan of immigrants,
Shy of man's splendour,
His fragility,
His transhumance,
His pollen,
Hoist to his own petard by the seed of his destiny,
By retaliation,
By the relation of man to woman on this earth
Be
He or she
From Mayo or Sind
And living in Leicester city,
Estrangement or harmony;
How it might be between a man and a woman;
The Deep Supermarket, next door to Ajay's.

The Murder of Harry Keyes

This was not a murder with a difference,
The murder of Harry Keyes at Racoo,
At Racoo in the night before his sweetheart's eyes
By two intelligence officers of the IRA,
Except that instead of issuing statements
Of 'widespread condemnation' and 'wholesale denunciation'
The bishops decided that deeds would speak more sincerely
   than words
And they went on an underwear strike
Outside the offices of the IRA in Londonderry and Belfast;
Stripping down to Y-fronts and tee shirts,
The bishops camped on the streets outside the offices
Of the IRA in Londonderry and Belfast.

Be it noted
That no statements of any kind whatsoever
Issued from the bishops
As they sat around in their dirty underwear
Puffing Woodbines and Silk Cut
And whenever an IRA man came in or out of the offices
A bishop in his underwear would say 'Howdee'
Without any expression on his face or intonation in his voice,
Just a plain 'Howdee';
Only imperceptibly reducing the tone
When it was evident that the IRA man
Was an intelligence officer of the West Fermanagh Brigade.

What an ennobling and selfless and poignant vocation it
   must be –
To be an intelligence officer of the West Fermanagh Brigade.

'Howdee,' the bishop whispered, 'Howdee',
And in the damp, dark, dank silence of the street

After twenty-one years the world's press begins
To take notice of something it has never noticed before.
'Howdee,' the bishop in his underwear whispers
Into the ears of the two IRA intelligence officers
Who murdered Harry Keyes at Racoo,
At Racoo in the night before his sweetheart's eyes,
'Howdee'.

Summer Holidays, Ireland, July 1989

in memoriam John McAnulty

Having dinner in The Noble Grape in Drogheda last night
– In the heatwave I had elected to treat myself –
I realised that I have been doing the same thing
For almost thirty years. For almost thirty years
In the shadow of the Boyne Viaduct
Doing the same thing, day in, day out.
Am I the same man as I was thirty years ago?
Sitting alone at a table for two in The Noble Grape,
I am not the same man as I was thirty years ago.
Thirty years ago I was dreaming of women
But although I am still dreaming of women
My dream has got more dream now in its dream,
More plural in its singular,
More butterfly in its caterpillar.

Summer nights I drive out to Mornington
And wallow in the estuary
And lie in the dune grass under the Maiden Tower,
Inspecting the navigation beacons twinkling in the dusk
And night crossing the bar.
Here I am sitting in The Noble Grape in Drogheda
And if I wasn't – would anybody notice?
On the other hand, I could be sunbathing
On the side of the road in South Armagh
With a bullet in the back of my head.
Either way, the greatest living editor in Ireland
Will not remember my name, or yours.

The Dublin–Belfast Railway Line

What I want is free rail travel
For the heroic democrats of the IRA.
What I want is to put them aboard
The Dublin–Belfast train for six months;
Have them travel up and down the line
Six times a day for six months.
I want them to get to know
All about trains, all about train travel.
I want them to get to know
Every embankment on the line,
Every landscape they have not deflowered,
Every bridge they have not groped,
Every wild hedgerow they have not
Buggered a virgin under.
I want the townspeople of every town
On the line to come out
At the stations and applaud our heroes
Go up and down the line,
Up the down line and down the up line.
I want the heroic democrats of the IRA
To enjoy the benefits of train travel:
The tenacity of luggage racks;
The cups of coffee at sixty miles per hour.
At the end of six months,
On the platform at Belfast Central,
I want to hear each of them
Swear an oath on a copy of *Mein Kampf*
To the unification of Ireland
With or without trains,
With or without passengers.

28 October 1989

Lord United Ireland, Christmas 1989

I

Peace
To your crackers.
Peace
To your plum pudding.

Each one of us has at least one affectation,
One convolvulus in bloom.
My father was chief of staff of the IRA
And *his* affectation was that he had *one* arm.
But I had *two* arms
And therefore grew up to believe
That a man with two arms
Was by definition inferior
To a man with one arm.

My solution
Was to insist that I had *three* arms,
As a consequence of which
I was stashed away in a psychiatric unit in Epping Forest
For three and a half years
With the help of money from my Fine Gael uncle
Who owns a chain of supermarkets in Middlesex
And his sister-in-law who is a nun in the Isle of Wight.

II

I was reborn in Epping
And since my return flight from Leeds–Bradford Airport
I have believed I have *eight* arms.
I live in a manger at the bottom of Kildare Street,
Tended to by the three wise women of Leinster House,
Carolina and Desdemona and Allanah,

61

With all their caravans of Camels & Opels, Gourds & Saabs.
In the word of the prophet Isaiah:
I am your local friendly Camel dealer.
I have come to prepare the way for the private motorist.

With my eight arms,
Lord United Ireland, they call me.
When I brandish my eight arms at them
They interrogate me: 'Are you United, United?'
'Are you Ireland, Ireland?'

Up and down the streets
Of Dublin and Belfast I go,
Octopus in search of his octopussy,
Flailing my arms, all eight of them,
Lord United Ireland.
You cannot see my head for my arms,
My snubby head.
My eyeless, mouthless, noseless head.
My blue bag of head.

III

As I make faces at you, this Christmas evening in Erin,
I am sitting in the window of the Dublin–Belfast train,
Ticking over at Semtex Station,
While bomb buggers pause from their bomb buggery to
    behold me
Juggling my cup of coffee from my fifth arm to my seventh
    arm,
The eight-armed juggler,
Lord United Ireland.

I have a high, as well as a low, opinion of myself.

Peace
To your crackers.
Peace
To your plum pudding.

At the Grave of O'Donovan Rossa, 1989

Not Irish merely but English as well;
Not English merely but Irish as well.

PART
IV

Around The Light House

I am swimming beside
A pregnant woman
In The Light House cinema
In Middle Abbey Street
In the city of Dublin.
We are watching a film
Entitled *The Navigator*.
A daydream is flowing
But the more it flows
The more scared I am
Of the pregnant woman beside me
And of the globe of her body,
The global message of her body.

Her boyfriend is swimming
The far side of her,
Licking a scoop
From an ice-cream tub.
I spotted the pair of them
On the Halfpenny Bridge:
I was enthralled by the enormity
Of her pregnancy
And by the fiction that she was holding
A Faber and Faber paperback in her hand.
Her boyfriend has a curly moustache
And he is sporting white jeans.
I try to restrain myself
From reaching out
And placing my hand on her tummy.
But I cannot restrain myself.

Yet when I do reach out

And place my hand on her tummy
She does not recoil from me
And her boyfriend is mining
Down into his ice cream.
On top of us on screen,
Pouring of copper
Into mould,
Gushes of orange,
White horse in a rowing boat.
I put my ear to her tummy
And tune into the film
Palpitating inside her.
I lay my ear on her navel
And hook into the soundtrack
Of a cast of trillions
Singing on a far shore,
Black-and-white in colour,
The farthest shore,
Under the farthest mountain,
Under the farthest sky,
Keening the lyric
Of the human city,
Auckland.

Her boyfriend leans across
And clamps a pair of earphones
On my head.
'Give me your head,' he mutters,
And I give him my head
And he takes it in his mouth
And sucks on it
And spits out a stone.
I adjust the earphones.
I can hear her baby breathing
In Dolby Stereo,

Her baby pilot
Grunting into his radar screen
As he fathoms the pip of my head.

I glance up at her head,
White flame of her brow,
In the floating studio
Of The Light House cinema.
I perceive a row of faces behind her,
A blackbird's chicks in a raspberry bush.
Her beak wide open, her eyes shut,
Projector Cat waiting to pounce.
I rise to my feet in slow motion
And bend down to her in her tip-up seat
And deliver her baby in a caesura of water,
In a red wedding of blood,
In a Mass of hands.
What can you not say in film?
Oh the Ming dynasty.
Oh the shoes of the fisherman's wife.

II

Oh the Ming dynasty.
Oh the shoes of the fisherman's wife
Are some damned good neighbour's borrowed sandals.
When *The Navigator* ends
I wait until the last credits go up
And the last sheep bleats
And the last bleat lip-reads me
And The Light House is empty.
As I dawdle to ponder,
A sailor in the exit says Thank You.
I rub my finger down along his jersey.

In front of me a tiny old lady,
More punting than walking,
Poles her way down The Light House steps.
She speaks to me without looking at me:
'This is not the first time I have seen this film
And it won't be the last.'
'But today is the last day' – I say to her –
'We have seen the last screening.'
'You are a pathetic middle-aged ram' – she replies –
'That you should believe in such finite facts.
Do you not see by the light of the half-moon,
By the light of The Light House,
By the light of your own fluids,
That there are no facts and that nothing is finite,
That the blue sky is not blue?'

Outside The Light House I stop
To stare up at the moon.
While I am staring
She paddles off between my legs
To catch the last bus home,
The number 39 to Stoneybatter,
The oldest stone road in Auckland,
From Tara to Glendalough.
Tonight she is going to give birth
At the age of sixty-seven,
Blood trickling from the corners of her mouth
As she climbs into bed on her own,
Into her king-size bed,
Purée of loneliness,
To be squeezed out
Onto the floor on her back,
Supine, prone,
The floor of her room,
Her room of her own

In the city of Dublin,
Where she knows no one
And no one knows her,
And be found in the blue
By-and-by by the janitor,
In her pair of tiny hands
A prayer book clasped, seemingly
A Faber and Faber paperback,
The Navigator
By Vincent Ward,
Inscribed with the words –
Affection, from Griffin.

Am I her only boyfriend?
Is he her only pilot?
In reality fiction is all that matters
And at the heart of it
The reflection of the earth on the moon's surface
Is mostly sea water,
Sea water mostly
In Middle Abbey Street
In the city of Dublin
Around The Light House.

PART
V

NIGHTS IN THE
GARDENS OF CLARE

to Kay Sheehy

A dialogue between two lovers, Soledad and Donal: Soledad, the daughter of a ship's captain, is a survivor of the Armada wreck the *San Marcos*, which went aground at Lurga Point, County Clare, in September 1588; Donal Thornton is a local Clareman and silversmith.

SOLEDAD   Our ships fell out of the sky at Malbay.
Street gangs of reefs slit our keels from heel to
    throat
At Lurga Point and Doonbeg.
Fat seas flung us up onto the jet-black shore.
Oh the coasts of Clare are black, black, black.
Thousands of natives stood there inspecting us,
Their eyes gleaming at the prospect of plunder.
I picked myself up off the sand, ready to die.
They stripped me naked and hung masks of
    devils
From my buttocks and they painted faces on my
    breasts,
With marker pens they drew eyes on my breasts,
The native Irish are obsessed with heads,
The native Irish are all heads, or rather,
They see themselves as being bodiless heads,
Their men are so full of their own heads
They think they have brains in their private
    parts.
They tied my hands behind my back
And pointed to a tower and a gibbet on the hill.
As I staggered towards it I glimpsed your
    nephew
And threw myself on his mercy.
He pulled me into his breast and he put
His mantle round me, concealing me
In that instant – it all happened
Quicker than an eyeblink – and I was safe

In the nest of his breast.
Safe in the wingspan of his cloak.
Let me be clear as the skyline of Clare,
The treeless skyline of Clare.
I did not lust for nor flirt with your nephew,
I simply asked him to rescue me and he did.
It was necessity that gave birth to Adam and
    Eve.
It was necessity that brought me and Donal
    together.
We are creatures of necessity.
Necessity is the mother of Love.

DONAL   It is exactly as Soledad has said, no less, no
    more.
It was not her deep beauty as a Spanish Lady,
Believe it or believe it not,
That drew me to her, but her cry for help.
Early that morning I was at work in my
    workshop,
Hammering out silver brooches in the shapes of
    the plants
Of the Burren –
Irish Orchids – Pyramidal Bugles – Bear Berries –
When Miko Vaughan and Nacey Considine,
T. J. Minogue and Franky Spellissey,
Arrived in to say that there were Spanish ships
Falling out of the sky at Doolin and Doonbeg.
'Let's go over and watch the ships
Breaking up on the rocks,' cried Nacey.
'It'll be surely great crack
Watching the ships breaking up on the rocks.
There's nothing like a disaster – a good
    shipwrecking –
To cheer the heart on a late September day.

Besides, there'd be the hangings,
And you'd meet people, like, hanging about at
the hangings.'
There were thousands of spectators at Lurga
Point,
Doolin and Doonbeg,
Watching the ships breaking up;
I lay on the cliff edge munching grass,
Watching the ships breaking up.
The soldiers – the joint militias of the Irish and
English –
Were hacking the heads off Spanish survivors;
The white horses of the waves were bleeding to
death.
Clare's trendiest film maker was there,
Boethius Clancy,
As famous for his wenching and boozing
As for his film making – a big bearded lout
In dark glasses and sleeveless black leather
jacket,
Parading up and down the seafront at Doolin
With a loud-hailer in one hand, and a leg of a
chair in the other.
When I asked who was the leather-clad, yellow-
haired lady on his arm
Someone said: 'That's his KitKat.'
She was Swedish from Nottingham, Minnesota.
She was heard to bleat:
'Eat me, Boethius, eat me.'
I got up off my face and ran down
Onto the rocks to where the survivors
Whose heads had not been hacked off
Were being rounded up, stripped,
And marched in lines to Tromra Tower.
It was then I saw Soledad fall towards me.

SOLEDAD   Necessity drew us together,
Nights in the Gardens of Clare.
Day by day we grew together.
Love fell upon us like a bird of prey.
With the help of the Northern Irish
In Antrim and Scotland
We will escape to Salamanca and a new life,
Never to return to this haunted country.
I will miss only the hills of Clare,
The Burren and Mount Callan;
Above all,
The Heights of Ennis where I found a home
In front of a shop called Epicene.

DONAL   Oh I will meet you *on the Height*, Soledad;
I will sit beside you *on the Height*, Soledad;
I will come to you *on the Height*, Soledad;
I will mince pies with you *on the Height*, Soledad;
On the Height we'll watch the world go waltzing
    by;
On the Height we'll watch the heads go marching
    past;
On the Height we'll read the *Clare Champion* and
    the *Hot Press* too;
On the Height we'll listen to the colour of the
    crack;
On the Height we'll listen to what they're saying
About us – even if it isn't very true:

'They had a mad one last night on the Height';
'She's got cool boots, that Spanish One';
'But he was really polluted and so was she';
'They're having a party tonight in Corrovorin.'

'Will I see you down in Brogan's later on?'
'Will I see you in the Auburn later on?'

80

'Will I see you in Dillinger's later on?'
'Or will I find you later on in the Old Ground?'

I saw a Pair of Reindeer in O'Dea's.
It was you.
O Soledad.

SOLEDAD O Donal,
Once in Ennis there was a Pair of Ears.
It was on the Height that I first saw the Pair of
    Ears.
As fine a Pair of Ears you've never set eyes on,
That is – until God put a Head between the Pair
    of Ears.
From that day on, the Head took over.
It was the Head all the way,
Head, Head, Head, nothing but Head,
And up in O'Dea's Bar on the hill
Instead of the Pair of Ears in the corner
There was the Head in the corner,
The Head with a head under his arm.
What could I do but go home to Spain,
Grieving for my lost Pair of Ears?
A Pair of Ears I first met in Ennis,
A Pair of Ears on the Height of Ennis.

DONAL Your breasts are in my eyes, O my love,
Nights in the Gardens of Clare;
O my love, O my river-swallowing sea,
Nights in the Gardens of Clare.

SOLEDAD *Si*,
And here is my hymn to my de Valera,
My Spanish Clareman, my Clare Spaniard.
There is no reason why you, de Valera,
Should not shed your puritanical plumage
And become, as once you were with Sinéad,

Gay and festive, carefree and frisky –
All that is most truly Spain, most truly Clare.
Preside outside the Courthouse
Over the courting couples round your statue,
With *bodhráns*, pipes and fiddles round your
     feet.
For I have seen the young virgins of Ennis
Holding hands with their fellas
On benches round your statue and your plinth,
But your eyes are always shut, thin obdurate
     man.
Open your eyes, behold your children free
To stay at home, work at home, play at home,
Nights in the Gardens of Clare.

On a good day I wake and hear
The River Fergus at my window
But on a bad day, and the bad days are many,
I wake and see far down below me
The coast of Doolin, black as black can be;
The black, black, black coast of Doolin;
I am falling, falling, falling,
Into the black, black, black coast of Doolin.

The rocks of Doolin are waiting to gnaw me.
The cliffs of Moher are waiting to guzzle me.
The shores of Malbay are waiting to spew me.
My father's ship, the *San Marcos*,
Breaks up on the reefs of Lurga Point
To the caterwauling of the laughter of the Irish,
All that scorn and derision,
All that greed and gluttony,
And the screams and pleas and howls of the
     souls of the drowning Spanish;

O Donal Thornton
                    I want to die

In your arms tonight;
                    let me die
In your arms tonight,
                    O Donal Thornton.

DONAL   Soledad, you're so far away from home.
         Come away with me to Corcomroe and I will
         Love you among insects who will protect you –
         The Confused, the Burren Green, the
            Anomalous,
         The Pearl-Bordered Fritillary, the Little Blue,
            the Beautiful Brocade.
         Come away with me to Corcomroe and with me
            pray
         At the altar of the three-light window;
         Was ever a tale so believable, yet so tall,
         As the tale of the Universe seen through a three-
            light window?
         At the Hub of the great Wheel of Fate,
         An infant child seen through a three-light
            window.

SOLEDAD Our Lady of the Fertile Rock,

DONAL   Have mercy on us.

SOLEDAD Our Lady of the Puzzled Forehead,

DONAL   Have mercy on us.

SOLEDAD Our Lady of the Running Stream,

DONAL   Have mercy on us.

SOLEDAD Our Lady of the Homeless,

DONAL   Have mercy on us.

SOLEDAD Our Lady of the Travelling People,

DONAL   Have mercy on us.

SOLEDAD	Our Lady of the Spanish and the Hungarian and the Ethiopian and the Palestinian Refugees,
DONAL	Have mercy on us.
SOLEDAD	Our Lady of the Northern Irish,
DONAL	Have mercy on us.
SOLEDAD	Our Lady of the Southern Irish,
DONAL	Have mercy on us.
SOLEDAD	Our Lady of the Pure Smile,
DONAL	Have mercy on us.
SOLEDAD	Our Lady of the Addicted to Death,
DONAL	Have mercy on us.
SOLEDAD	Our Lady of the Glow of Life,
DONAL	Have mercy on us.
SOLEDAD	Soledad, you're so far away from home.
DONAL	Come away with me to Poulnabrone and I will Hold you in my arms, in your skintight Blue jeans and your skintight white jumper, Like the priest holding up the Eucharist at Mass, The skintight white wafer of the Host with blue feet. I will put you standing on the capstone Of the Portal Dolmen of Poulnabrone And you will open your arms wide to the white-hot sun So that your breasts will sing to the points of the compass, Your breasts will be as tuning forks quivering, Your breasts will be voices in the white-hot sun,

Voices with their nipples audible.
Your breasts will sing innately to all men of
     peace and goodwill
And the world will be free.

SOLEDAD   Soledad, you're so far away from home.

DONAL   Come away with me to Corofin and I will hide
     you
Under the weir, under the weir,
In Bankyle House beside Lake Inchiquin,
There to sleep, wake, walk, read in silence and
     peace
In the company of Rose and George and
     Donough.
I will tell them you are coming to stay with
     them,
Rose and George and Donough;
Under the weir, under the weir,
In Bankyle House beside Lake Inchiquin.
After the war is over, after we have all died
And have been born again, over and over, born
     again over and over,
There will be a time for loving and a time for
     smiling.

SOLEDAD   Soledad, you're so far away from home.

DONAL   Come away with me to Lissycasey and at Fanny
     O'Dea's
I will pour an egg-flip down your slipper-red
     throat,
An egg-flip to beat all egg-flips;
Not even my own dear mother could beat
An egg-flip such as Fanny O'Dea can beat.
After egg-flips at Fanny O'Dea's
We will ride on white horses

Across the red islands of Ennis
To the green airport at Shannon,
A frozen jet on runway number 3,
A trembling hare crouched
To fly you back to your Spanish shore,
The Mountains of your Dread,
And the Coasts of Barcelona;
And the Coasts of Barcelona.

PART
VI

Amnesty

I

The perimeter wall of a prison presents a problem
To a small boy,
Particularly if he is nine and a half
And he does not know, and nobody is ever going to tell him,
That when he was born, he was born in prison,
A confinement within a confinement.
Pardon? Pardon.

II

As he drives past the prison, Daddy does not explain –
'That's the prison.' If it was any place else
He'd spin around from the driving wheel and explain –
'That's the Rotunda Maternity Hospital'
Or 'That's the Wellington Monument'
Or 'That's the Four Courts.'

I swivel about in the back seat of the car,
A pair of small boy's eyes splattered all over the prison walls.
The prison is a blocked-up keyhole.
Its gates do not deign to speak to me.
They despise me.
Its barred cells do not deign to speak to me.
They despise me.
A grey, granite, waistcoated pile of sarcasm –
Like my arrogant, alcoholic big brother
The day he vomited into the fireplace.
Pardon? Pardon.

Each time we drive past the prison
– Which is four times a day –
I can see through its walls.

The prisoners' faces are decked out in vomit.
I am dejected that Daddy does not name it.

He who is the great namer of things;
For whom the names of places and people
Are the signs by which he teaches me
That they are holy and precious;
That the plankton of all human life is mercy.

Perhaps it is that a prison is not a holy and precious place –
A place that does not have a name.
Perhaps it is that prisoners are not holy and precious people –
People without names;
That the plankton of all human life is mercilessness.

III

I lie awake in bed at night fretting about the prison.
The headlights of passing cars toss shadows on the ceiling
That are cell bars. There are no faces.
But then the face of the Pope is projected onto the ceiling,
The Supreme Pontiff is appearing on the balcony of St Peter's.
I ask myself: When the Vicar of Christ's
Standing out there, explaining things to the world,
What does he make of the bars across his eyes?
How is it that I've never seen him put out his hands
And, falling to his knees,
Clench those bars fiercely, helplessly?
Yet Jesus is the patron saint of all prisoners
Because he was a prisoner himself,
Not a special-category prisoner
But a prisoner like the rest of us,
One of three.
Today you will be with me in paradise.
Pardon? Pardon.

Daddy puts his head around the bedroom door and whispers,
'Are you all right?'
I tell a lie and answer him:
'Yes, Daddy, I am all right.'
But I am not all right. The prison is all over the ceiling
And I am hiding from it down under the sheets.
The pink vomit of my big brother's sarcasm is all over my
    face.

IV

Against Daddy's wishes I courted a black girl,
A medical student from Cape Town.
'The most beautiful city in the world,' Daddy groaned,
Sobs of fury in his throat.
He put me out of the house and told me never to come home.
He loved me as no man ever loved his son
But he said to me – crisply, glassily, over the breakfast table,
Over the cornflakes and the marmalade – 'Don't ever come
    home again.'
Pardon? Pardon.

I went to another country and to a far place,
A mining village in northern Ontario,
A dark new habitat in oblivion,
And I freed myself from the dream of being his favourite son
And I found peace of mind in the company of my wife,
In the lovingkindness of her bed.
We have four boys and a girl, the youngest,
Whom we named Amnesty – after a radio programme
We'd heard, about people who write letters to prisoners.
It was the word, and the acoustic of the word:
Amnesty.
The etymology of the word:
Amnesty.

All participle, all verb;
Oblivion;
Like holding hands behind a waterfall;
Like a lake-dwelling on stilts in deciduous forests;
Like a nest caught up in a weir in a river in spate;
Like traffic lights at red when there's no traffic at night.

v

On winter nights when she's playing ice hockey on Main
   Street
I like to put my head out the door and call out her name –
Amnesty.
It's so fortified, yet vulnerable, and it falls away
Or gathers itself to itself
Like a yard of deer bunching
In an open space at the tree line
Or between telegraph poles on a wet day.
'It's getting late, Amnesty, it's getting late.'
When I behold her racing back down the street to greet me
What I feel is a sense of zero:
Amnesty.
It is such a swift and shedding spectacle to see her face
Peering out at me from its fur hood,
Its nimbus of expectancy with serrated edges,
All frills,
Oblivion,
And to hear myself reiterating her name –
Amnesty.

Pardon? Pardon.
It is such a delight to reiterate her name
– Amnesty –
That I cannot pronounce it often enough
– Amnesty –

And after we've made love
My wife puts me back down into sleep,
Oblivion,
By seashelling into my ear the lullaby of our daughter's name:
Amnesty
In the key of A minor
Into the seashell of my ear, the lullaby of my fate –
Amnesty.

PART
VII

DADDY, DADDY

Ulysses

I am hiding from my father
On the roof of Joyce's Tower
In Sandycove.
He is downstairs in the gloom
Of the Joyce Museum
Exchanging euphemisms with the curator,
The poet Michael Hartnett,
Meteorological euphemisms,
Wet and cold for June.

I am standing at the battlements.
I am eighteen years old.
The battle is whether or not
He will buy a copy of *Ulysses*.
It is a battle about money
But it is a battle also about morality
Or 'morals' as it is called.
It began this morning at the breakfast table
When I asked him for twenty-one shillings
To buy a copy of *Ulysses*.
He refused on the grounds that on top
Of it being an outrageous sum of money
Which a poorly paid judge could ill afford,
It was a notoriously immoral book.
Even the most liberal-minded Jesuits
Had condemned *Ulysses*
As being blasphemous as well as pornographic.
My mother jumped around from the kitchen sink:
'Give him the money for the wretched book
And let the pair of you stop this nonsense
For pity's sake.
Will we ever see peace and sense in this house?'
My father stormed out of the kitchen,

The *Irish Independent* under his arm:
'I'll not be party to subsidising that blackguard
Bringing works of blasphemy into this house.
In the year of Our Lord nineteen hundred and sixty-three
I will not be an accessory to blasphemy.'

I caught the 46A bus out to Joyce's Tower,
Newly opened as a museum.
The curator offered to share with me
A carafe of vodka left over
From a literary soirée of the night before.
It was the day after Bloomsday.
Monday, June 17, 1963.
We sat in a compatible silence,
Contemplatively, affably,
Until upheaval of gravel
Eradicated reverie.
I rushed to the door and glimpsed
My father at the foot of the iron steps.
I climbed up to the roof, hoping to hide
From him up there in the marine fog,
Foghorns bleating in the bay.

I hear footsteps behind me and I know it is he.
He declares: 'I suppose we will have to buy that book.
What did you say the name of it is?'
I tell him that the name of it is *Ulysses*.
I follow him down the staircase and he submits:
'Mr Hartnett, I understand
You stock copies of a book entitled *Ulysses*.
I would like to purchase one copy of same.'
'Certainly, Your Lordship, certainly,'
Replies the ever-courteous, Chinese-eyed curator.
When from his wingbacked chair behind his desk
He takes from a drawer

A copy of the jade-jacketed *Ulysses*,
The Bodley Head edition,
My father asks him if he would have brown paper
With which to wrap the green, satanic novel,
Make a parcel out of it.
The curator peers into a wastepaper basket
'Made by the Blind',
As if peering down into a bottomless lift shaft,
Casts a funicular, questing second glance at my father
Before fishing out crumpled bags of brown paper
Which the night before had ferried bottles of vodka.
He lays them out on the desk top
And smoothes them, taking pains
To be obsequiously
Extra punctilious, extra fastidious.
Formally he hands it over to my father,
As if delivering to some abstract and intractable potentate
A peace gift of a pair of old shoes.
My father pronounces: 'Thank you, Mr Hartnett.'
The curator, at his most extravagantly unctuous, replies:
'Very glad to be able to oblige you, Your Lordship.'

My father departed Joyce's Tower with the book.
The next day when I asked my mother if she'd seen it
She said it was in their bedroom beside my father's bed.
Her bed was beside the window and his bed
Was between her bed and the wall.
There it was, on his bedside table,
Ulysses,
With a bookmarker in it – a fruitgum wrapper –
At the close of the opening episode.
When a few weeks later
I got to reading *Ulysses* myself
I found it as strange as my father
And as discordant.

It was not until four years later
When a musical friend
Gave me my first lessons
That *Ulysses* began to sing for me
And I began to sing for my father:
Daddy, Daddy,
My little man, I adore you.

Study of a Figure in a Landscape, 1952

after Francis Bacon

– Did your bowels move today?
– Yes, Daddy.
– At what time did your bowels move today?
– At eight o'clock, Daddy.
– Are you sure?
– Yes, Daddy.
– Are you sure that your bowels moved today?
– I am, Daddy.
– Were you sitting down in the long grass?
– I was, Daddy.
– Are you telling me the truth?
– I am, Daddy.
– Are you sure you are not telling me a lie?
– I am, Daddy.
– You are sure that your bowels moved today?
– I am, Daddy, but please don't beat me, Daddy.
  Don't be vexed with me, Daddy.
  I am not absolutely sure, Daddy.
– Why are you not absolutely sure?
– I don't know, Daddy.
– What do you mean you don't know?
– I don't know what bowels are, Daddy.
– What do you think bowels are?
– I think bowels are wheels, Daddy,
  Black wheels under my tummy, Daddy.
– Did your black wheels move today?
– They did, Daddy.
– Then your bowels definitely did move today.
– Yes, Daddy.
– You should be proud of yourself.
– Yes, Daddy.

- Are you proud of yourself?
- Yes, Daddy.
- Constipation is the curse of Cain.
- Yes, Daddy.
- You will cut and reap the corn today.
- Yes, Daddy.
- Every day be sure that your bowels move.
- Yes, Daddy.
- If your bowels do not move, you are doomed.
- Yes, Daddy.
- Are you all right?
- No, Daddy.
- What in the name of the Mother of God
  And the dead generations is the matter with you?
- I want to go to the toilet, Daddy.
- Don't just stand there, run for it.
- Yes, Daddy.
- Are you in your starting blocks?
- Yes, Daddy.
- When I count to three, leap from your starting blocks.
- I can't, Daddy.
- Can't can't.
- Don't, Daddy, don't, Daddy, don't, Daddy, don't.

The One-Armed Crucifixion

after Giacomo Manzù

How many thousands of hours on the shore at Galway,
In the drizzle off the back of the sea,
On the sodden sands,
Did we spend hurling together, father and son?
Pucking the sliothar, one to the other,
Hour in, hour out, year in, year out.
How many thousands of times, old man,
Did you strike a high ball for your young son
To crouch, to dart, to leap,
To pluck the ball one-handed out of the climbing air?

Fjord

You were Abraham but you were also Jesus.
In your Jesus suit
You liked to teach for the sake of teaching.
You were a teacher before you were a judge.

You'd descend with a word like 'fjord',
By the light of the standard lamp
On a winter's night in firelight,
Savour it, bless it, deposit it on my tongue.

'Fjord' – you'd announce – 'is a Norwegian word.'
I'd gaze up at your icicle-compacted face
As if you'd invented Norway and the Norwegian language
Especially for me.

You'd confide that we had fjords of our own in Ireland
And the noblest of all our fjords was in County Mayo,
The Killary fjord in the safe waters of whose deep, dark thighs
German submarines had lain sheltering in the war.

Look into your Irish heart, you will find a German U-boat,
A periscope in the rain and a swastika in the sky.
You were no more neutral, Daddy, than Ireland was,
Proud and defiant to boast of the safe fjord.

Crinkle, near Birr

Daddy and I were lovers
From the beginning, and when I was six
We got married in the church of Crinkle, near Birr.
The *Irish Independent* photographed the wedding.
My mother gave me away.
My sister was best man.
He was forty-two and a TV personality in Yorkshire,
Close to his widowed mother in Mayo,
Always having his photograph taken,
Always grinning and polite and manly and coy and brittle,
Checking the stubs of his chequebooks,
Tying up his used chequebooks in elastic bands,
Putting money away for a rainy day,
Making gilt-edged investments.
It was in the days before he became a judge.
He compèred boxing fights and women's beauty contests
In an accent that was neither English nor Irish nor American.
It was known as the Athlone accent.
When he spoke of Athlone
Listeners were meant to think
Of a convent in the middle of a dark forest
To which the speaker was chaplain.

We went on our honeymoon
To Galway, the City of the Tribes.
We stayed in the Eglinton Hotel in Salthill.
For breakfast we ate grapefruit segments and toast
And the manager bowed, the waiters goosing around us.
We stood on the Salmon Bridge counting
Squadrons of salmon floating face down in the waters below,
Waiting to go upstream to spawn.

In the afternoons we spawned our own selves in our hotel
    bedroom

Listening to cricket.
The West Indies were playing the MCC at Lord's.
We lay in bed listening to Rohan Kanhai batting for a double
   century
And Garfield Sobers taking six wickets for forty-five runs.
O Owen of the Birds,
That is what it meant to be Irish and free –
To be father and son in bed together
In a hotel in the City of the Tribes
Listening to cricket on the BBC Radio Third Service.
After dinner we walked on the pier at Spiddal,
Holding hands, watching schools
Of porpoises playing in the apple-light of the Western sea.
One night after dinner we drove to Gort,
Where Daddy let his hair down
And we played a game of cricket
In the back garden of another father-and-son couple.
When Daddy bowled, I was his wicketkeeper.
He fancied himself as Ray Lindwall
And I fancied myself as Godfrey Evans –
Godders jackknifing over bails and stumps.
When we returned to the hotel, we entered
By the fire escape, feeling in a mood to be secretive,
Black iron staircase flicked up against white pebble-dash
   gable.
Daddy divided the human race
Into those who had fire escapes and spoke Irish
And those who had not got fire escapes and did not speak
   Irish.
Another night we sat in a kitchen in Furbo
With a schoolteacher hobnobbing in Irish
Exotic as Urdu, all that rain and night at the windowpane.

The marriage lasted five years.
On a summer's night in Newcastle West

After a game of cricket with boys my own age
I came back into the house without my school blazer.
'Where have you left your school blazer
Which you should not have been wearing in the first place?
School blazers are not for wearing.
School blazers cost money.'
I had left it on a fence in the field.
When I went to retrieve it, it was lolling out of a cow's mouth,
One arm of it.
Daddy took off his trousers belt,
Rolled it up in a ball round his fist,
And let fly at me with it.
In a dust storm of tears I glimpsed
His Western movie hero's eyes stare at me.

When I was twelve, I obtained a silent divorce.
Ireland is one of the few civilised countries
 – And the only country outside Asia –
In this respect, that while husbands and wives
Can only at best separate,
Children can obtain a silent divorce from their parents.
When I look back at the years of my marriage to Daddy
What I remember most
Are not the beatings-up and the temper tantrums
But the quality of his silence when he was happy.
Walking at evening with him down at the river,
I lay on my back in the waters of his silence,
The silence of a diffident, chivalrous bridegroom,
And he carried me in his two hands home to bed.

The Persian Gulf

The skylight is our escape route in the event of fire.

At night after supper we kneel on the floor
Of the dining room and recite the Rosary in Irish.
Kneeling with my elbows in a dining room chair,
My skull ensconced between the two arms of a carver,
I dream of the Persian Gulf and try
To imagine what the skylight would look like
On fire but I can no more visualise it
Than I can visualise the prayers we are saying
In a language in which we do not converse
And which is as strange to me as French or German.
Praying in Irish to a skylight on fire is an abstract art.

Abstract Art was in Ireland long before Abstract Art.

As the great Ferris wheel of the Rosary
Monotonously revolves on a winter's night
I am borne away on the wings of prayer
And I see our three-storey house going up in flames,
57 Dartmouth Square,
And Daddy in his blue-and-white striped pyjamas,
With the cord tied in a dicky bow over the fly,
Gripping the stepladder
While we clamber up the fire escape to safety.
As we stand on the roof of our burning house
We are speaking Irish to one another as to the language born.

The fire-brigade engines, having charged
Through the city streets blaring their klaxons,
Assemble in the street below to feed up their ladders,
Spool them out to us sliding down the slopes of the rooves.
Daddy stands by a chimneypot, admiring the night sky,

Looking like Danny Kaye in *The Court Jester*
And putting his arms around my shoulders,
With that Connemara *blas* of his he says to me ruefully,
'It is a fine, bright night to be abroad.'

When the first fireman reaches us
And cries to us – 'Are you all right?' –
Daddy says to him in Irish: 'We don't speak English.'
The fire-brigade man, barely visible in smoke,
A pair of horn-rimmed spectacles on his gaunt, lean face,
All black helmet and black gauntlets,
Shrugs his eyebrows and climbs back down the ladder.
The ladders are retracted and the fire engines driven away,
Leaving us to burn to death speaking Irish.

Next morning, except for the crows in the trees
And the ruins of the house sticking up through the waters,
It is all quiet in the Persian Gulf,
A skylight on fire floating upstream.

Breakfast

after Renato Guttuso

Having served Daddy his breakfast
Of porridge and tea,
Placed the morning newspaper in his hands,
The *Irish Independent*,
Mother in her white silk slip and chapped bare feet
Nestles her head on the kitchen table and folds her arms.

I sit in silence listening to her snoozing,
Him slurping.
What is it in a beast that after a night of lovemaking
He eats his oats over black banner headlines
Of assassination, coronation and war?
I get up from the table and snatch the newspaper from his
    hands
And fling myself down at Mother's feet,
Licking with my wet frantic tongue her hot silk sides.

The Company of the White Drinking Cauldrons

I was the only creature in the world Daddy trusted,
Which is why in later years he conspired to murder me.
He was a member of a secret society
Which met in the crypt of a Unitarian church,
The Halla Damer,
On the west side of St Stephen's Green,
Next door to the Winter Garden Palace.

The society was known as
The Storytellers' Union or
The Company of the White Drinking Cauldrons.
All the storytellers
Hailed from the Gaeltacht.
While Bartla Ó Conghaile was speaking
I stared in awe at his Kikuyu lips,
Asking myself –
What is it about these men and women
That their voices are in their eyes?
That at the portal stones
Of their cheekbones
Peer sentinels of repose?
'Suaimhneas' – a woman whispered to me,
Bending down low over me,
Goosepimples on her breasts,
Her kelp-scented breasts.

Midnight, the proceedings over,
Daddy wrapped me up in his cloak
And walked me home.
We were two riderless horses after midnight,
Walking up the middle of the street
And I slept in my clothes standing up.
All I could decipher in my bedroom mirror
Were my nostrils quivering, my sweaty flanks.

Lifesaving

after Francis Bacon

Having served my apprenticeship in tree climbing in Mayo,
I climbed up onto the roof of our Dublin home
By the banks of the Grand Canal
And knelt down at the skylight over your bedroom,
Feeding my nose into its pane of clear glass.
I could see you but not hear you.
Mother was reclining on her back on the carpet,
Kicking her legs in the air.
You dived between her knees,
Snaked your hands under her back,
Put down your head into her shoulder
And she locked her arms around your neck.
I could see her laughing with her eyes closed.
Not since the night of my twelfth birthday,
When she permitted me to take her
To the film of *War and Peace*
In the Adelphi in Middle Abbey Street,
Henry Fonda as Pierre,
Audrey Hepburn as Natasha,
Had I seen her look so inconsolably delighted – that anarchic
     smile
Of hers, so characteristic of her clan,
The MacBride clan
Of Antrim and Mayo.
Between the chimneypots
A barge was sliding past.
Back down in the kitchen after tea
Offhandedly I asked you what you'd been doing.
You replied without looking up from the table,
A chord of peremptory surrender in your voice:
'Your mother was teaching me lifesaving.'

114

The Martyrdom of Saint Sebastian

after Andrea Mantegna

Once a week you light
On Sunday afternoon
After Sunday fourball,
Or mother lights,
A fire in the drawing room.
After putting practice on the carpet
Into a metal contraption made in England
You preside in your Ethiopian armchair
By a piece of furniture known as 'The Bookcase'.

'The Bookcase' has glass doors and it is locked.
But I know where you keep the key.
We dwell in a conspiracy of keys.
I gawp through the panes at the spines
Gazing out at me through their prison bars,
Especially your own two heroes' spines,
Oscar Wilde and Roger Casement,
Of whom in later years
If any suggestion of impropriety be made
You protest truculently
It is all a British conspiracy.
No matter, you are not deterred
From espousing that most British sport,
Golf, until it has displaced your wife
And kids, and you abandon us
For a place in the rain in Troon,
St Andrews, Royal Lytham St Anne's,
Calling yourself by another name,
Jack Nicklaus, Arnold Palmer, Bobby Jones,
Bobby Locke, Max Faulkner, Sam Snead.
While I dreamed wet dreams of Glynis Johns

You swooned at the sight of Bobby Locke's plus fours
And Max Faulkner's socks.

The end of the world has come and gone
But you remain standing on the eighteenth tee,
Driving for hole, match, championship.
I behold you at the top of your swing,
Black-gloved left hand over right,
The club gripped parallel to the ground,
Your chin tucked into your left shoulder,
Your hips swaying with such passivity
Your slacks are shimmying in rainlight
And melting, your windcheater unzipping
Of its own volition, your creamy torso
Revealed to us in embalmed puberty,
Virgin flesh bloodied with love bites
Whose arrowheads are tipped with lipstick,
And your eye is not on the ball
As we had thought but gazing heavenwards.
Your hips go down again, undulate,
Your loincloth sagging under weight of sweat
And gore, your true vocation
Extending downwards to a bouquet of knees.

Crouched down under the tee in the rough grass,
Divots leapfrogging past me in the dark air,
I cry out, not 'Daddy, Daddy',
But 'Sebastian, Sebastian,
Why has thou abandoned me?'
Everything is a pretext for something else.
But I would if I could
Unfreeze the frame where it stopped at pain.
May not Saint Sebastian step down, hit his drive,
Pitch his next shot pin high, hole his putt?
Still he will perish from the dream of love.

Apartheid

When after twenty-seven sessions of Electric Convulsive
    Therapy
I was discharged from hospital in London,
I got the night train from Euston to Holyhead,
Sipping baby gin-and-tonics in my empty carriage,
Savouring the consolation of the passing night,
The invisible emptiness of the universe.
Daddy and Mummy met me at seven-thirty next morning
Off the boat train at Westland Row.

Driving home through the deserted streets of Dublin,
None of us could think of anything to say
Until outside the National Maternity Hospital
Daddy imparted to me that in the afternoon
He and I would be attending the Rugby International
Between Ireland and South Africa.
Our cousin, it seemed, was playing in the front row
Of the scrum for Ireland,
Propping up the scrum for Ireland.

As I sit in the East Stand freezing,
All the men of Ireland with rugs on their laps,
Whiskey flasks in their hip pockets,
I ask Daddy why there are no black men
On the African team.
'Apartheid' – he answers authoritatively – 'Apartheid.'
He pronounces the word 'Apartheid'
With such élan, such expertise,
With such familiarity, such finality,
As if it were a part of nature,
Part of ourselves.

I try to remember what Apartheid is.

I cannot remember what Apartheid is.
Odd to think that only this day last week in London
I was having my twenty-seventh session of Electric
    Convulsive Therapy
While today I am sitting in the East Stand in Dublin
Watching an African team with no black men
Playing an Irish team with all white men,
Daddy's arm around me, his chin jutting out.
If I was a black man, I would play for Africa.

Sport

There were not many fields
In which you had hopes for me
But sport was one of them.
On my twenty-first birthday
I was selected to play
For Grangegorman Mental Hospital
In an away game
Against Mullingar Mental Hospital.
I was a patient
In B Wing.
You drove all the way down,
Fifty miles,
To Mullingar to stand
On the sidelines and observe me.

I was fearful I would let down
Not only my team but you.
It was Gaelic Football.
I was selected as goalkeeper.
There were big country men
On the Mullingar Mental Hospital team,
Men with gapped teeth and red faces,
Oily, frizzy hair and bushy eyebrows.
Their full forward line
Were all over six foot tall
And fifteen stone in weight.
All three of them, I was informed,
Were suffering from schizophrenia.

There was a rumour
That their centre-half forward
Was an alcoholic solicitor
Who in a lounge bar misunderstanding

Had castrated his best friend
But that he had no memory of it.
He had meant well – it was said.
His best friend had had to emigrate
To Nigeria.

To my surprise, my relief, my delight,
I did not flinch in the goals.
I made three or four spectacular saves,
Diving full stretch to turn
A certain goal around the corner,
Leaping high to tip another certain goal
Over the bar for a point.
It was my knowing
That you were standing on the sideline
That gave me the necessary motivation –
That will to die
That is as essential to sportsmen as to artists.
More than anybody it was you
I wanted to mesmerise, and after the game –
Grangegorman Mental Hospital
Having defeated Mullingar Mental Hospital
By 14 goals and 38 points to 3 goals and 10 points –
Snorting your approval, you shook hands with me.
'Well played, son.'

I may not have been mesmeric
But I had not been mediocre.
In your eyes I had achieved something at last.
On my twenty-first birthday I had played on a winning team,
The Grangegorman Mental Hospital team.
Seldom if ever again in your eyes
Was I to rise to these heights.

Mother's Boy

I

You bought a racehorse
In your barrister days
And called it after me –
Mother's Boy.
It was a chestnut colt
And I recall dark days
Of delight in the 1950s
Bringing water to the red horse.

It won nothing
And cost you money –
Like me.
If you could live your life again
Which would you choose,
Your racehorse or me?
You'd choose your racehorse
And so would I.
Horses are spiritual animals
Whereas poets are neither
Spiritual or animal,
On average a bit of both
In a grey self-indulgent way.

II

After ten days of narcosis,
Acceptable animality,
Sleep, food, excretion,
I wake up and they order me
To get out of bed, put on
My clothes, and get ready
To go for a walk with my father.

You take me for a drive
In the Dublin mountains,
You at the wheel
Of the Vauxhall Wyvern,
Me in the horsebox
That once belonged
To Mother's Boy.
We stop and sit on a ditch
Overlooking the city.
There are no little fairy folk,
No little Celts,
Peering over the walls at us.
I contemplate the cut of your jib
Through buttercup and fern,
Your resemblance to Mussolini,
Mussolini topping his egg,
Your admiration of him,
That look of penetration,
That set of the jawbone.

You tell me calmly, sympathetically,
That you would like to kill me,
That at twenty-one years of age
I do not know the difference
Between 'can' and 'may',
That my grammar is appalling.
I gaze out at Dublin Bay
And begin to laugh.
'What are you laughing at?'
You ask me angrily.
'Don't be angry, Daddy, it's just
That I know that I'm not a horse
And I'm a little bit anxious.'

Back at the hospital
You hump me into the ward on your back,
Past the television cameras
Making a social-conscience documentary.
They put me back into bed
For another ten days of narcosis.
'Don't be angry, Daddy, it's just
That I know that I'm not a horse
And I'm a little bit anxious.'

1966

I have been eight months
In the leucotomy ward
Of a mental hospital
In Epsom –
Epsom of the thoroughbreds.
It is Sunday afternoon.
I have got a pass-out
With the man in the next bed,
Terry Hardwick,
A British Army paratrooper.

Training with the SAS,
Terry cracked up.
He is a big, dreamy, creamy,
Curly-headed lad
With a black dog temper.
We decide to visit
Friends of his in West Croydon,
A middle-aged couple in a semi-d,
Cliff and Cheryl.
When Terry was small
He used to live in a caravan
With Cliff and Cheryl
In Cheshire.
'Those were the golden
Days' – Terry admonishes me –
'The days before socialism
Destroyed Olde England.
If only Germany
Had won the war.'
Do I know that Hitler
Went to grammar school?
It was socialism
That did for Hitler.

Cliff and Cheryl are chirpy
With pop music titbits;
The current hit
Of the charts,
'The Eve of Destruction'
By Barry McGuire.
All afternoon we listen
To it again and again,
'The Eve of Destruction'
By Barry McGuire.
We cannot have enough of it,
'The Eve of Destruction'.
The chat is mostly
About the Moors Murders,
Myra Hindley, Ian Brady.
Cliff and Cheryl
Do not see eye to eye
About the Moors Murders.
I enquire where is the toilet.
'Top of the stairs, Paddy,
Straight ahead.
There's no traffic lights
But you'll find it, Paddy.'

As I stand over
The lavatory bowl,
In the small bath to my left
There is a scuffling noise.
I glance to my left.
Downstairs I settle in again.
Cheryl is saying
That the Moors Murders
Might have been an accident
And Terry agrees with her.
Everyone knows that children

Can be right little monsters.
For something to say, I say:
'I see you keep a pet
In the bath upstairs.'
Cheryl smiles bashfully:
'That's Peter,
Our baby alligator.
When we want a bath
We go next door.
We have good neighbours,
Don't we, Cliff?
In the summer we keep
Peter in the back garden,
We feed him cats,
Don't we, Cliff?
Dead cats and live cats.'

Back in the leucotomy ward,
Lying on my back in my trolley bed
Before lights out,
In my striped pyjamas,
Listening to Terry
Chewing bubble gum
(And to David Brown pacing
The ward in black flippers;
He covers two miles a day
Pacing the ward in black flippers,
He never speaks, there is a spectre of a
Grin somewhere between his nose
And his mouth, his eyes
Have a moist, dark cast,
He has two big dimples,
One each side of his forehead,
Two voluminous crannies)
I grip tight the headrail

Behind my head
To stop myself screaming,
So tight I can feel
My knuckles whitening.
I dream of my father.
Who is my father?
Will I ever see him again?

Birthday Present

On my twenty-third birthday
It was showery
With sunny intervals.
You asked me
To walk into town
With you.
On the bridge over the canal
You smiled as if God
Was a lighting cameraman
Secreted in a Georgian
Doorway on Leeson Street;
As if mortality
Was a divinity
Glimmering under a lintel.

The still waters of the canal,
The great lock gates idle as cattle,
The plane trees along the towpath,
These were your deities.
You paused on the crest
Of the canal bridge
To take in the view
Of Charlemont Bridge
To the west
And Baggot Street Bridge
To the east.
Down Leeson Street
We strode out
A brick gorge
Past The Kiosk
And The Singing Kettle.
Through sunlight and rain
We did a fling through the Green.

At the top of Grafton Street
You instructed me to wait outside
The Radio Review Record Shop
While you did a message inside.
As I sheltered in the doorway
Of the Radio Review Record Shop
From the next shower,
A noted Fine Gael politician
And Irish-speaking economist,
From the suburbs of Clontarf,
In a belted mackintosh
Passed by without seeing me,
A young man with grey hair
And steel-framed spectacles
And under his grey slacks with turn-ups,
Polished black leather boots,
Known in his party as Brian Boru.
I had seen him the night before
At a party in Fitzwilliam Square.
He had had another man lasso him to a chair
And beat him up with a silk cravat,
Chanting 'Long Live Brian Boru'.

When you came back out of the shop
You handed me an LP record
In gift wrappers, mumbling Happy Birthday.
When I told you I had seen
The noted politician
Your face melted with pride and admiration
That such an upstanding young man,
And an economist too,
An Irish-speaking economist,
Was a flower of your party.
At home in my bedroom
I unwrapped your gift.

It was The Beatles' new LP,
Sergeant Pepper's Lonely Hearts Club Band.
When I ran back downstairs to you, you said,
Your voice streaky with awe:
'Did you ever think of politics as a career?'
'Dad' – I said – 'thank you for the birthday present.'

Stellar Manipulator

Judge Durcan, you wanted
Your eldest son to be a lawyer.
But wanting always to be
Like the other you, Daddy,
To become your understudy,
I became at the age of twenty-five
Stellar Manipulator
At the London Planetarium.

When I went for the interview
With the Director of the Planetarium,
John Ebdon,
He so much looked
And sounded like you
I had to be careful not
To address him as Daddy.
'I hear that you write
Poetry' – he exclaimed.
I winced. He continued:
Many a night I saw the Pleiads,
rising through the mellow shade,
Glitter like a swarm of fire-flies
tangled in a silver braid.
When I failed to identify
The author, he said
'Tennyson' – and gave me the job.

II

Seven a.m. on a black Sunday morning
In Ladbroke Grove.
The black telephone. Your black voice.

131

'This is Harrow Road Police Station:
You are requested to act as bailsman.'
Down at the station at 7.45 a.m.
The duty officer takes down details.
Status: Married. *Sex*: Male.
Nationality: Irish. *Age*: 25.
Occupation: Stellar Manipulator.
The duty officer focuses his eyes
And asks me to repeat my occupation
That he can note it down correctly.
I say it with deliberation,
Pronouncing solemnly each syllable:
'Stell-ar Man-ip-ul-at-or.'
He smiles as you used smile, Daddy,
If ever there was so much as the remotest
Rumour of humour in the universe,
A smidgen of light in the black.

III

Back home in Dublin
In the locker room of the golf club,
When other members of the fourball
Enquire after your eldest son,
Knowing that I am the black
Sheep of the family,
Thinking to get a rise out of you,
'Well, what's he working at now?'
You take your time,
Scrutinising the clay adhering
To the studs of your golf shoes,
Scraping it off with a penknife.
Your rejoinder is indifferent,
Laconic, offhand:
'He's a –' satisfactorily

Flaking off another lump of clay,
'Stellar Manipulator.'

The Two Little Boys at the Back of the Bus

The two little boys at the back of the bus,
You and I.
Where would we have been
Without my mother?
As well as being my mother
She was your mother also.
All you and I were able for
Was playing Rugby Football
Or swooping up and down the touchline
Shrieking at one another
To maim or kill our opponents.

We were Jesuit boys,
Sons of peasants
Who played a burgher's game
Which was called Rugby Union,
The ideology of which was to
Enact in the muck and lawn
Of the playing fields of Ballsbridge
A parody of homosexual aggression:
Scrum, hook, tackle, maul.

We thought it right and fitting,
Manly and amusing,
That our clubs were named
After barbarian tribes.
You played for the Senior Vandals,
I played for the Junior Visigoths.
Our life's ambition was to play
For the Malawians
Against the Springboks
In Johannesburg,
Drinking lager,

Putting the boot in,
Taking the boot out.

After the game
And the whooping-it-up
Of male bodies
In the showers,
The boisterous buttocks,
The coy penis,
The Jesuit priest with a box camera
Lurking outside the cubicles,
The ex-missionary
Father A'bandon with an apostrophe.
You and I always got dressed
Ahead of the rest
To bag the back seat first.
We were always, you and I,
The two little boys at the back of the bus,
Going home to Mother.

Safe in the back of the bus
At seventy-two you share your biscuits with me,
Your packet of digestive biscuits,
As we head back down the Stillorgan Road
To Mother.
Mother will meet us at the bus station
And drive us out to the plane
Which she will pilot herself,
A Fokker 50.
When we are safely ensconced
At an altitude of seventeen thousand feet
Turning left at Liverpool for Preston,
She will come back down from the cockpit
And put us both to sleep
With an injection of Sodium Amytal.

Isn't that what we've always yearned for,
Father and Son,
To be old, wise, male savages in our greatness
Put to sleep by Mother?

Susannah and the Elders

after Ludovico Carracci

When I came home with the good news that I was going to
    get married
Daddy telephoned my future mother-in-law requesting her
To stop the marriage. When she confided in him
That she was inserting an engagement notice in the *Irish Times*
He demanded that his own name be omitted
In order that it would read that I was the son of my mother
But not the son of my father.
On the wedding day he refused to attend,
Standing, as he said, on principle.

After our children were born, he consented
To recognise our marriage, and he began
To make visits alone to us to dandle them on his knee,
He was daft about them, and my wife sat up in her bath
    laughing
And he began to fall in love with my wife – old badger that he
    was
He had an eye for the warm, wise woman.
He knew that warm, wise women grow only on trees
And are not to be found in the Dublin social round.

But when he asked for her hand through the bathroom door
I had to wave the mat at him. 'Daddy,' I remonstrated,
'I love you but you cannot have my wife.'
After he had consulted with my mother, I heard no more
    about it
And he went back to his law books and he rarely emerged
    from his sett
Except to dig up old stones and scrape their surfaces.

When my wife used finally evolve from the bathroom
In a bathrobe and a wet towel round her ox-blood hair,
She'd find him on his hands and knees at the bathroom door,
Digging up old stones, scraping their surfaces.
She'd pick him up in her arms and stroke him on the nape of
his neck
And let him paw her. She admired him
For what he was – apart from me, the loneliest creature she
knew,
A man alone.

The Mayo Accent

Have you ever tuned in to the voice of a Mayoman?
In his mouth the English language is sphagnum moss
Under the bare braceleted feet of a pirate queen:
Syllables are blooms of tentativeness in bog cotton;
Words are bog oak sunk in understatement;
Phrases are bog water in which syllables float
Or in which speakers themselves are found floating face
    upwards
Or downwards;
Conversations are smudges of bogland under cloudy skies.
Speech in Mayo is a turbary function
To be exercised as a turbary right
With turbary responsibilities
And turbary irresponsibilities.
Peatsmoke of silence unfurls over turf fires of language.

A man with a Mayo accent is a stag at bay
Upon a bog rock with rabbits round its hooves.
Why then, Daddy, did you shed
The pricey antlers of your Mayo accent
For the tree-felling voice of a harsh judiciary
Whose secret headquarters were in the Home Counties or
    High Germany?
Your son has gone back to Mayo to sleep with the island
    woman
Who talks so much she does not talk at all.
If he does not sleep with her, she will kill him – the pirate
    queen.

Poem Not Beginning with a Line from Pindar

Having photocopied Goya by moonlight, the IRA
Hijacked a minibus on a circular road
In Armagh of the Nightingales,
Tromboned ten Protestant workmen into lining up
Along the footlights of the Armagh hills,
To kick high their legs, look left, look right,
And fed them such real midnight jazz
That not even Goya on a high
Could have improvised a tableau
Of such vaudeville terror, such prismatic carnage,
Bodies yearning over bodies,
Sandwich boxes, Thermos flasks, decks of playing cards.

Next morning at breakfast in the kitchen
I enquire of Daddy his judgment.
The President of the Circuit Court
Of the Republic of Ireland,
Appointed by the party of the Fine Gael,
Scooping porridge into his mouth,
Does not dissemble as he curls his lip,
Does not prevaricate as he gazes through me:
'Teach the Protestants a lesson'
And, when I fail to reciprocate,
'The law is the law and the law must take its course.'

'Teach the Protestants a lesson',
That's what the man says,
The judge says,
The President of the Circuit Court
Of the Republic of Ireland says.
If you are puzzled,
Dear Oxford University Reader in History,
What it shows are not lacunae

But black holes
In your encyclopaedic knowledge
Of the roots of fascism in Ireland.
The party of the Fine Gael is the party
Of respectability, conformity, legitimacy, pedigree,
Faith, chivalry, property, virility,
The party of Collins, O'Higgins, O'Duffy, Cosgrave,
Great men queuing up at the bride's door.
Walk tall to the altar rail in pinstripe suit and silk tie.
Talk the language of men – bullshit, boob, cunt, bastard –
And – teach the Protestants a lesson.
The law is the law and the law must take its course.

Dovecote

The black dog temper of the Durcans
Was notorious in Keelogues and Turlough;
The landlord riding out on his horse
From his saddle by your father clutched,
Dragged to earth.

After your mother gave birth to you
On the side of the road
She crawled out of the ditch
To a dovecote in the meadow,
The columbarium of the Big House.
She stared up from your floury, bloody, shut-eyed kittentorso
And saw 12 circles of pigeonholes,
12 pigeonholes in each circle,
144 doves beating their wings.

All the days of your life
You brooded about eviction.
Why were you so angry with life?
Eviction.
Why were you so hard on us all?
Eviction.
Why always did you invoke the name of Michael Davitt?
Eviction.
Why in Straide did you always stop the car?
Eviction.
Why always did you stare at the tree where the house once
    stood?
Eviction.
Why did you begin every journey an hour early?
Eviction.
Why did you worry about everything always?
Eviction.

Why did you worry your mother into her grave?
Eviction.
Why did you stitch your money into your trousers belt?
Eviction.
Why did you hate landlords?
Eviction.
Why did you become a landlord yourself?
Eviction.
Who was the first landlord?
The Lord God in Heaven was the first landlord
And he was a Gentleman Farmer in Mayo.

Today I stand in the same deserted dovecote
– Grey day, black skies –
Staring up at your evicted face about to be cremated,
Staring up at your multifarious faces in their pigeonholes,
All 144 of them,
Their 288 wings beating in vain
The flames of the landlord's ovens.
Evict: Why do priests eat gods?
Evict: Why do gentlemen commit genocide?
Evict: Do doves eat doves? Souls souls?

Antwerp, 1984

We are keeping silent vigil at the window
Of the train from Amsterdam to Brussels,
Sitting opposite one another,
An agèd judge and his middle-aged son,
Shooting the dykes
Into flashfloods of oblivion
At the bottom of a vertical sky.
We are travelling at speed
Through the suburbs of Antwerp.
I am staring at a poplar tree
Quivering in a November breeze
When I glimpse your face in the window
And you glimpse mine.
In the high-speed window
Our eyes meet, each of us
Yearning for what the other yearns:
To be a tree – that tree.
By the time the message
Arrives in my brain
The train is a half-mile past
The level crossing
Where we glimpsed one another
In the poplar tree.
You elect to break the silence.
'My favourite poem' – you announce –
'Is "Trees" by Joyce Kilmer.'
'My favourite poem' – I reply –
'Is "The Brook" by Lord Tennyson.'
That is all we have to say
To one another.
I look at you
As you are
In your train seat,

Not as you were
A moment ago in the window,
Your own limbs are unleafing
And quivering
With Parkinson's,
All your roots
Heaped up in bundles
On your lap,
The dark floor beneath your feet
Gone, vanished.
You have five years to live.
I gaze up at your treetops
– Your glazed eyes underpainted with moonlight –
And I pledge that when they fell you,
While they will sell you for firewood,
I will give logs of you
To a woodcarver in Sligo,
Michael Quirke of Wine Street,
Butcher turned woodcarver,
Out of which to magic statuettes
Of the gods and goddesses of Ireland,
The Celtic Deities.
I will wash your body
In linseed oil and turpentine.
I will put you in the window
Of his butcher's shop in Wine Street.
I will call you by your proper name,
Mac Dhuarcáin,
Son of the Melancholy One.
As we approach the crossing of the Rhine
No man could look more melancholy
Than you – Melancholy Daddy.
God took out a Stanley Knife,
Slashed the canvas of life,
Called it a carving of your face,

Called it you.
As we crawl over the Rhine
I put my hand on your knee,
Your quivering knee,
The pair of us gazing down into the wide river far below.

Geronimo

Although we were estranged lovers
For almost thirty years,
When Daddy knew that he was going to die
He asked that we marry again.
After a reconciliation under a Scots
Pine in Palmerston Park
We remarried in the Church of St Aengus
In Burt, near Pluck.
In the navel of the Grianán of Aileach
We lay side by side on our backs
For the wedding photographs
Taken by a tall thin youth
With tresses of platinum grey hair
In a mauve suit and white sneakers.

We spent a second honeymoon
In the lakes of Sligo,
Putting up at the Ryan
Yeats Country Hotel
In Rosses Point,
A seaside hotel named after a poet
With special rates for families.
Throughout his life
Against all-comers
Daddy had maintained
That the lakes of Sligo
Were more scenic,
More bountiful, more placid,
More inscribed, more hallowed,
More inky, more papery,
More sensual, more ascetic,
More emblematic of what we are
Than the lakes of Killarney.

By the shores of Lough Arrow
In his eightieth year
At Ballindoon in the rain
In a two-light window
Of a roofless Dominican friary
He sat in profile
While I crouched behind a holly tree
Snapping him with my pocket Japanese camera.

By the shores of Lough Arrow
In his eightieth year
Among water-rolled stones with cranesbill
I spread out a tartan rug
For us to sit on and picnic
Listening to lakewater lapping,
Holding each other in one another's arms,
Resting our heads in one another's laps,
Hares springing up out of their own jackets.

For the umpteenth time
I told Daddy the story
Of Patrick Pearse's visit
To Daniel Corkery's house
In Cork city – the weather-slated
House by the Lough of Cork –
How Pearse solemnly informed Corkery
That the Lough's lakewater lapping
Had kept him from sleeping –
'A regrettable inconvenience,' coughed Pearse.

Daddy loved to hear me
Tell that story and he'd hoo-hoo-hoo
Like a steam train chugging through Tír na nÓg.
He'd snort, 'Tell me it again',
And I'd tell him it again

And it was part of our liturgy
Of courtship and romance and marriage
That I should leave out bits
So that he could take a turn also
In the storytelling – we were a pair
Of choirboys among the rocks,
Chanting in orgy on a summer's morn
Our girlish devotion to the rain.
In the Corkery story, Daddy's line
Was the name of Corkery's novel
That celebrates the weather-slated house,
The Threshold of Quiet.

By the shores of Lough Arrow
In his eightieth year
At the cairn of Heapstown
While I stood atop the capstone
Daddy lay down in the uncut grass
And curled up like a foetus,
An eighty-year-old foetus.
'What are you doing?' – I shouted down at him.
He made a face at me.
'Climbing goalposts' – he shouted back up at me.

By the shores of Lough Arrow
In his eightieth year
Among the passage graves of Carrowkeel
In the Bricklieve Hills
He sat down in the bog cotton
And gazing north-west to Knocknarea
And to Deerpark and to Creevykeel
And to Ben Bulben and to Classiebawn
He began to weep in his laughter.
He wrapped his long white hair
Around his shoulders and refused

To utter for the rest of the day.
That night by the light
Of a golden-sepia half-moon
We walked the cliffs at Rosses Point,
Hand in hand among the actual shells.
He cupped my ear in his hands and whispered,
'Geronimo'.
'I know,' I said, 'I know.'

By the shores of Lough Arrow
In his eightieth year
In the main street of Ballinafad,
In the only street of Ballinafad,
On the steps of the Castle of the Curlews
He stood, and shaking out his brolly,
'You Curlew you,' he said.
'But for the red perch in the black stream
My life has been nothing, son.
Be good to your mother.'

In the six months of white horses
Between our second honeymoon
And his deathdive
Geronimo's lovingkindness to me
Was as magnanimous as it was punctilious.
His last words to me were always,
'Be good to your mother – bring her
Flowers every day – what she likes
Above all is phlox.'
As we shook hands and kissed
In the doorway, waiting for the elevator,
He'd add: 'Don't be long.'
I won't, Geronimo, I won't – be long.

Bare Feet

'Be grateful, mind,
That you have shoes on your feet' –
You used warn me, reminding me
That in nineteen hundred and fourteen
You had to walk to school
In your bare feet:
Before daylight in the black, wet cold
Of a Mayo boreen
One and a half miles to National School
In your bare feet.

Shoes were the sole item of drapery
You deemed worthy of mention.
When I was forty-three years old,
In the year of your dying,
And I needed a new pair of shoes
You offered me an old pair of your own shoes,
Stately big black men o' war
With long, thin, twiney black laces.

When I demurred at wearing them
You were scandalised
That I would not step into your shoes.
At the end of your life
As all through your life
I scandalised you.
Should I have stepped into your shoes?
I should have stepped into your shoes.

Whenever I pass a shoe shop I stop
To look in the shop window for you.
I scan the shop window for you.
Whenever I see a man wearing a pair of shoes

And nothing else except a pair of shoes
I know it is you,
Old Bare Feet
From the Ox Mountains.

Once in the Ox Mountains
You were Young Bare Feet,
An Indian tinker boy
With a future flaming ahead of you.
After eighty years of walking
Up and down the world
You became Old Bare Feet,
An Indian elder tinker man
Burned out in Dublin city.
Daddy,
Every street is a tightrope
I see you balancing on
In your bare feet.

'The Dream in a Peasant's Bent Shoulders'

You are sitting on a chair
Upright, moulded plastic,
At the end of your hospital bed
In the seventy-bed ward.
'Where are my pyjama bottoms?'
You cry at me, with a hoe in your hand,
A small, split cry.
When I fail to answer you, you cry,
'What have they done with my pyjama bottoms?'
'I don't know, Daddy, I don't know.'

All I know
Is that you served the State
Unconditionally
For twenty-eight years
And that on this December afternoon in Dublin,
Without providing any reason or explanation,
They have taken away your pyjama bottoms.

Outside on Pearse Street
My mother weeps at the hospital gates.
Such was your loyalty to the State,
Your devotion and fidelity to the State,
You took Mother on one holiday only in twenty-eight years –
A pilgrimage by coach to the home of Mussolini
And Clara Petachi near Lago di Como,
A villa in the hills above Lago di Como.
Did you see in Mum your Clara?
Starlet, child bride, all negligée and tulle.

Loyalty to the State was the star
In the East of your life
And reward by the State.

Instead, they have taken away your pyjama bottoms
Leaving you only with your pyjama tops
And a hoe in your hand.
Your peasant's bent shoulders have ceased their dreaming
As you crouch down before me, a jewel in torment.
Out of willow eyes you stare at me.
'Hold my hand,' you whisper.

A blond male doctor struts brusquely past
As we crouch here holding hands in twilight.
'Hold my hand,' you whisper.
'I am holding your hand, Daddy,' I respond.
But you do not hear me.
Clinging to your hoe
And gripping tightly my hand, you scream:
'Hold my hand.'

The French Revolution

When I went to visit you for the last time
Your hair was so long that it swerved down to your waist,
You who had always worn your hair shorn,
Short-back-and-sides with a parting down the right,
And your fingernails were as long as a Paris mannequin's.
Your hair fell in long, lank, white strips down to your waist,
Your gaunt face veiled by it.
When you opened your mouth
I was not sure whether you were smiling or screaming.
I was not sure whether you were a man or a woman.
You sat upright on a plastic chair,
Your hands in the lap of your blue polka-dot silk dressing
    gown.
You were taking no notice of your surroundings –
Doctors, nurses, other people's visitors.

We sat in silence.
You were staring at something in the corner of the ceiling.
In the afternoon sunlight I was thinking
Of the Storming of the Bastille on the fourteenth of July
When you lurched forward and hit me in the face,
More of a tap than a hit,
Scratching my cheek with your fingernail.

The story of the French Revolution was your favourite story
When your children were small,
Before they got beyond the range of your storytelling,
Before they got lost in a world with no story.
You loved to tell about the downfall of Robespierre,
'The Seagreen Incorruptible'.
Your hero was Danton:
To overcome the enemies of the fatherland
Audacity is necessary,

155

Audacity again,
And always audacity.

As I flinched from your blow
The Storming of the Bastille went out of my mind
And I was gazing up into the white, frozen, riveted wastes of
    your face
As you gazed up at the guillotine about to fall:
You will show my head to the people
And my balls to Robespierre –
He has need of them.
When I asked you if you needed anything
You tried to hit me again,
A swipe that missed.
That was the last time, Daddy,
I saw you wholly alive.

Cot

We cringed around your bed in the hospital ward.
The matron announced you would die in half an hour.
She spoke as if dictating from a train timetable.
Always in Italy the trains run on time.
I was dispatched to telephone the relations
But visitors to the dying had access only to a payphone.
None of the family had any change.
I had to borrow two tenpenny pieces
From the matron who had scheduled your death.
The first payphone did not work but the second did.
The relations said they would be with us in no time.
When I came scuttling back into the ward
And peered over the shoulders of my brothers and sisters
I saw that the deathbed had become a cot
And that you, Daddy, were a small, agèd infant
Struggling to stay alive in the world.
You were kicking up your legs in the air,
Brandishing your bony white knuckles.
I realised that you were my newborn son.
What kind of a son will you be to me?
Will you be as faithful a son to me
As you have been a father?
As intimate, as funny, as alien?
As furry, as skinny, as flighty?

Old man, infant boy,
As you writhe there
On your backside
In your cot
How helpless you are,
A minuscule helplessness
Heaving with innocence;
A baby dinosaur

With an expiry date.
You begin to bawl.
My mother takes off her black glove
And lays her hand
Across your threadbare skull.
You wave her goodbye,
She who loves you
After one day
And forty-four years.
You go back to sleep,
The black world to rue.
Bonny boys are few.
Don't fret, son,
Don't ever again fret yourself.

Glocca Morra

Dear Daughter – Watching my father die,
As one day you will watch me die,
In the public ward of a centre-city hospital,
Mid-afternoon bustle,
A transistor radio playing two or three beds away,
Paintwork flaking on the wall,
His breath dwindling,
His throat gurgling,
A source disappearing slowly,
Source of all that I am before my eyes evaporating,
Well, watching your own father die slowly in front of you,
Die slowly right under your nose,
Is a bit like sitting in the front row of the concert hall
Watching a maestro performing Tchaikovsky's Grand Piano
    Sonata.
It's spectacular, so to speak,
But the audience feels helpless.

When Daddy died
I wrung my hands at the foot of his bed
Until a consultant doctor told me to stop it
And to show some respect for the dead.
The old prick.
He had done nothing for Daddy
Except pollute him with pills for twenty years
For fees in guineas.
They threw a sheet over him
And put screens around the bed
But I stood my ground
At the foot of the bed
While the transistor radio,
Like something hidden in a hedgerow,
Went on with its programme –

Rosemary Clooney crooning
'How are Things in Glocca Morra?'

Outside the ward window
– Which was in need of cleaning, I noticed –
The sun was going down in the west over the Phoenix Park
Where Daddy and me
('Daddy and I' – he corrects me –
He was a stickler for grammar),
Where Daddy and I
Played all sorts of games for years,
Football, hurling, cricket, golf, donkey,
Before he got into his Abraham-and-Isaac phase
And I got the boat to England
Before he had time to chop off my head.

O Daddy dear –
As we find ourselves alone together for the last time,
Marooned in this centre-city hospital public ward,
I think that there is something consoling – cheerful, even –
About that transistor playing away in the next bed.
The day you bought your first transistor
You took us out for a drive in the car,
The Vauxhall Viva,
Down to a derelict hotel by the sea,
The Glocca Morra,
Roofless, windowless, silent,
And, you used add with a chuckle,
Scandalous.
You dandled it on your knee
And you stated how marvellous a gadget it was,
A portable transistor,
And that you did not have to pay
A licence fee for it,
You chuckled.

A man not much known for chuckling.
The Glocca Morra,
Roofless, windowless, silent and *scandalous*.

Rosemary Clooney –
The tears are lumbering down my cheeks, Dad –
She must be about the same age as you,
Even looks like you.
I bet her handwriting
Is much the same as yours.
You had a lovely hand,
Cursive, flourishing, exuberant, grateful, actual, generous.
Whatever things are like in Glocca Morra
I'm sad that we're not going to be together any more.
Dear Daughter – If and when the time comes
For you to watch me die,
In a public place to watch me
Trickling away from you,
Consider the paintwork on the wall
And check out the music in the next bed.
'How are Things in Glocca Morra?'
Every bit as bad as you might think they are –
Or as good. Or not so bad. Love, Dad.

On the Floor at the Foot of the Bed

The pyjamas Daddy died in –
St Bernard, Dunnes Stores, 100% Cotton,
Extra Large, To Fit Chest 43–44,
Do Not Soak, Re-Shape While Damp –
I have no problem about wearing them,
No more than you have a problem
About wearing the nightdress
That your mother died in.
It is a little nightdress,
A little ball of white cotton,
And besides, it will not be long
Until I will be ripping it off
Your small, frail body,
Rabbitroutes behind your ears,
And you will be ripping
Daddy's pyjamas
Off my own small, frail body,
Rabbitroutes behind my ears.

I will toss your mother's nightdress
On the floor at the foot of the bed.
You will toss my father's pyjamas
On the floor at the foot of the bed.

While they jostle on the floor with seeming passion
We will jostle with clumsy tenderness upon the pillow.

Mortuary

When you were laid out in the mortuary,
Put on display, mounted and framed,
In an open coffin on trestles,
Before they lidded you,
And we all filed in
For five decades of the Rosary,
Halfway through the 'Our Father'
A lady in a fur coat
Flew in the door
– A spurt of hairy-hemmed saliva –
And she stood in front of us,
Right up close beside you,
Belladonna at your nose tip.
I observed the smile on your lips.

After the last 'Glory Be
To the Father' had been mumbled
And as we all began
To shuffle out into the night
To climb into the mourners' cars
With our little white hands
In front of our little black suits,
She whispered to me: 'Leave me
Alone with your father.'

When I turned around in the doorway,
Sideways under the lintel,
To salvage one final glimpse of you,
I saw that she was wearing a blue bikini
Whose brassiere was studded with emeralds.
The smile on your lips was subtle.
You seemed to be saying to her:
'You have unbuttoned your fur coat.'

She whispered to you: 'My Lord,
For you I have unbuttoned my fur coat.
In all the years to come of oblivion
Never again will I button up my fur coat.
For you my fur coat will remain always open.'

Bank Clerk

There is no justice in life
But in your court there was justice
And the price of it
Was loneliness –
Loneliness that became a circus legend
In Circuit Court mythology
With your own family tagging along behind
In a caravan painted black on black
With the letters RIP in white.

While you ran the fairest court
In all of Connaught
Your family rested in peace.
For fear of being prejudicial
Or being seen to be prejudicial
You had the exquisite fingers
Of your hyper-sociable nature
Amputated, and locking yourself away
In hotel bedrooms, you declined
To visit even your own relations
In their home across the street
From the courthouse.

When you were made to retire
After twenty-eight years on the bench
– They were afraid that in old age
You might relax into wisdom,
'No Buddhism on the bench,' minced
Your national socialist handlers –
You sat out the remaining years
On a bench in your bedroom
In red-eyed loneliness;
The obedient hound

Of your hair lying down
In a coma at your feet.

You were a great judge
Because you were a great clown.
In a wig and gown
You were the biggest act in Connaught.
Not any old wig and gown
But a wig and gown festooned with chains.
In chains from neck to ankle
You felt attired to deliver
The balanced verdict;
And you did.

In the treetops of your top-storey apartment
You crouched at your bedroom door
Like a grey squirrel, gnawing at it
Until you had gnawed a loophole in it,
Just as I three miles away across the city
In my bunker with no windows
Like a rat had gnawed a loophole
In my own act.
Once a month with your pension cheque
You took a bus down to the bank,
Just as I once a month
Took a bus to the unisex hairdresser's
To feel a woman's hand upon my skull.

You could have had your cheque
Paid directly into your account
But by having it mailed to you
You had a pretext.
You took a bus down to the bank,
Deliberately forgetting to bring
Your chequebook with you, thereby

166

Obliging the bank clerk to talk to you,
To confirm your identity, to look up
Your bank account number, to repeat it,
To tap into her computer terminal
And caress your identity, fondle your identity.

You rejoiced to stand at the counter,
Gazing through the hatch at the face of the bank clerk,
Her young shelly face framed by the hatch,
Just as a half-dozen shop fronts down the street
I rejoiced to recline before the looking glass,
Gazing up at the coiffeuse caressing my scalp.
She'd smile at you and your red eyes
Would turn blue and your lips quiver
And your nostrils itch
And you'd make no attempt to be businesslike,
Content to stand there at the well of her face,
Supping smiles from the well of her face,
Chewing the cud at the fence of her spectacles,
Swishing your tail in the face of the customer behind you.

When the priest – like a striptease-show impresario –
Flicked the electric button
To release your coffin onto the rails
That would trundle it into the cremo
– Into the fiery furnace with the dainty pink curtains –
There was a solitary bouquet of loose flowers on the coffin
    lid,
White freesias
Left there by the bank clerk.
The men in peaked caps were afraid to remove them
When they removed the chrysanthemums and carnations and
    cards.
They were afraid to remove them because they were loose
From your bank clerk,

A solitary bouquet of loose white freesias,
All your haloes, Daddy, blooms
On the black and ivories of a grand piano
In the apartment of the unknown woman.

Kierkegaard's Morning Walk in Copenhagen

after Tony O'Malley

Outside the crematorium, listening to men
Being sensible and not talking about their feelings
About Daddy having been a moment ago incinerated
And exchanging informations about the afternoon's rugby
    fixtures
– 'Is it today Blackrock are playing Old Belvedere?' –
And their wives discussing the menu for luncheon
– Mushroom soup, leg of lamb, meringue with chocolate
    sauce –
Stamping my feet and swinging my arms,
I spot my father in the porch of the crematorium,
Putting on his top hat, waiting for a lift.

He looks so doll-like, vulnerable, cuddly;
Bandy-legged little judge
In green frock coat and black topper,
His head barely measuring up to the stomach
Of the important lady he's chatting to,
Barely measuring up to her navel,
Her gold filigree navel
Inlaid with treacle of ebony.
'Always poking his nose into other men's wives' groins.'
Oh the simple malice of the respectability.

With a black Bic Biro I scribble a note to him,
Scurry across the tarmacadam and hand it to him:
'A Memento for your Hatband' – I shout to him and he smiles,
Barely measuring up to her navel,
And taking off his top hat he inserts it in his hatband.
It reads in my father-like-son handwriting:
'Purity of heart is to will one thing.'

Sitting up in the back of my uncle's Opel Kadett,
I can see Dad still standing in the porch
Of the crematorium, waiting for the man
With the ash bucket to come and take him away.
He is taking on and off his top hat
And taking my note in and out of his hatband,
Holding it up to the light and scrutinising it,
Blushing, the colour of virtue,
Apparently finally putting it back into his hatband.
The ashman slams down his bucket and folds his arms
While Daddy once more yet again takes off his top hat,
Barely measuring up to her navel,
To pluck out of his hatband a by-now familiar tune:
'Purity of heart is to will one thing';
Her gold filigree navel
Inlaid with treacle of ebony.

The Children of Lir

after Hugo Simberg

My half-brother and I
Are two small brutes in hard hats.
We go up and down the world
Taking pot shots at nesting swans.
We carry a stretcher that has no body in it,
Nor canvas,
Just the two bare poles.
I go in front and he comes behind.
We serve bog and mammon.

One wet July day when golfers
Ruled the world and you, Daddy,
Were a man in your prime,
We arrived at the seaside links
With our stretcher and we put
A white blindfold over your eyes
And tied it around your head,
Your long strawberry-blond hair galloping down your cheeks,
And we gave you a gift of a bunch of dead daisies
As a thank-you gift
For bringing the pair of us into the world.
We put the two poles into your palsied hands
And we carried you across the Halfpenny Bridge
On your last journey past the golf course,
Ducking our heads under golf balls,
To the city reservoir at Poolaphooca
Where in the Ice Age you delighted to picnic.
There, at the Well of All Souls, we drowned you.

Daddy, Daddy – O Wounded Angel –
When will you deploy your wings?

When will you see that all your sons are brutes?
When we turn the next corner into Leeson Street
You will fly away, won't you?
Under a double-decker bus, under a bread van,
Under a milk lorry, under a dray,
Into the canal in whose still waters you will
Sit still for all eternity, ricocheting,
Protecting us:
Black eyes, white wings, orange beak, down, neck, soul.

Chips

I am sitting alone in the window of the Kentucky Grill,
Staring out at O'Connell Street in the night,
Shoving chips into my mouth.
Girls in paper hats are mopping up floors all around me.
Presently they are mopping up my feet.
'Excuse me' – I listen to myself say to them
As I hold up my feet to accommodate their mops,
Shoving a last chip into my mouth.
On the bin at the door it says:
FEED ME.

When Daddy died I gazed upon his chips
– I mean, his features –
While a priest poured a bottle of ketchup over him.
I thought it strange
And I walked out of the hospital into the city of night.

When I was seven and he took me to see
Charlie Chaplin in *City Lights*
In the Regal Rooms,
After the film was over we walked all the way home
From Hawkins Street to Leeson Street
Through streets that were dark and wet and cold and
    homelier
Than any landscape I was to see again,
Until after your death to Newfoundland I came
To give one quick, brief,
Received-in-boots-of-woolly-warmth-
By-fishermen's-wives
Recital of my verses.

There is no one in my life
Whom I disliked so submissively,

Yet whom I loved so mercilessly,
As you, Daddy. To me
You were at once saint and murderer.
When you raised your right hand
To smash in my face,
I saw the face of the murderer.
When you spoke the name
Of a belovèd townland or parish,
Keelogues or Parke,
I saw the face of a saint.

You were the artist of artists,
Ur of the Chaldees;
Priest of priests,
Melchisedech of the Ox;
Storyteller of storytellers,
Homer of Nephin;
Piper of pipers,
Carolan of the Moy;
Poet of poets,
Raftery of Turlough.
That's it –
I've had my chips.

Micky Donnelly's Hat

I'm in Baku, Micky, in Azerbaijan,
And by God, Micky, I'm in trouble.

Faïf – a small, round, middle-aged Mussulman –
A little barrel of a gentleman the hoops
Of whose years have humbled him –
Is twirling his worry beads.

He's worried because he's got me on his hands.

What he does not surmise
Is that I've got beads –
My father's beads –
My father's wine-dark Rosary beads –
In my jeans pocket,
And twined in perspiration
My fingers are around them clenched.

When Daddy slipped on the ice,
I salvaged his Rosary beads from the bin,
The black bin beneath the windowsill.
I carry them about with me wherever I go,
Such as now, Micky, in Baku,
A spot of bother in Baku,
Where to the north the Caspian Sea is aflame
With oil derricks – a gallows for every wave –
While to the south, it flows – becalmed, as it appears –
Onto the Iranian shore.

Will the sins of the sons
Be visited on their fathers, Micky?
It is the same
In Baku as in Belfast.

But so long as grown men
Can sit and twirl their worry beads
– Worry beads that were once their fathers' worry beads –
There is a pixie of hope, is there not?
Only today an old lady came hobbling into the local teashop
Enquiring hopefully after her lost pixie;
She cries out between the counter and the door –
'Has anyone seen my pixie?'

Micky, I like it that you wear your own hat at an angle
As I like to think I do mine.
In Baku Airport,
As in Belfast Central,
I pray to my father and I begin to discern
The profile of a smile glow in the ruins of his eyes.
When you're an Azerbaijani in Belfast
You don't stop twirling your worry beads.

Exterior with Plant, Reflection Listening

after Lucien Freud

No day could be more normal than today,
Wednesday the thirteenth of September 1989,
Twelve noon in O'Connell Street and I am standing
Across the street from the Oisín Kelly sculpture of Larkin,
At the number 13 bus stop outside Broadway Amusements
With a bunch of flowers in my hand, chrysanthemums and
    gladioli,
My glamorous mother, aged seventy-four last week,
Telling me about how Daddy played in 1938
A game of golf with Mussolini in Milan
In the Garden of Fascism Golf Club.
I am thinking how on a normal day like today
You notice things you do not normally notice:
The boy sitting beside a pram of apples
Has his arms folded, thinking of something else;
He has had his hair permed;
The girl parking her car in a no-parking slot
While she rushes the Pass Machine of the Bank of Ireland;
She also has had her hair permed.
How usual, how normal, how everything is,
When a small, red-haired, baby-faced man
Accosts me, and standing before me,
Gapes at me in a frenzy.
When I look as if I am about to ask him
What does he want, he howls at me:
'My wife and daughters are admirers of yours
But I have to tell you that I am not
An admirer of yours.'
He stamps off across the street
With a self-righteous strut, tying up
His scarf in a self-righteous knot.

On the other side of the street he looks back to check
That he has had the desired effect.
My mother beside me laughs that crazy laugh of hers
That is her birthmark. I gaze up into the arms
Of Larkin – the more she laughs.
And laughs. 'Your father was like a child.'
I take out my pocket camera and snap her
And when I get back the print from the camera shop
It is the most elegiac photograph ever taken of my mother,
A face on the wind, all epic and ephemera,
And over her shoulder you can see a man with a pocket
    camera,
His reflection,
In the passenger window of a passing Nissan Bluebird.

The Repentant Peter

after Francisco de Goya

Tonight is my forty-fifth birthday –
You are two years dead.
Last thing I do before getting into bed
Is kneel down beside bed
In my Marks & Spencer's women's pyjamas
Which I purchased thinking they were men's pyjamas,
A womanless man on a shopping spree.
Laying my head in my hands on the bed
I give thanks for the gift of life,
For your authorisation of me,
Your retrieval of my future,
An ape seeding himself in the rift valley.
I ask for forgiveness for my sins.

First time my wife saw me
Kneel down beside bed
She ate my head off
She was that shocked.
I do it
Because that is what you taught me to do.
I could not
Not do it.
You taught me that like you
I am destitute animal,
Frailer
Than plump lamb under candlelit chestnut,
Frailer
Than mother cat wheezing in cartwheel,
Frailer
Than galaxies of geese,
And that behind all my sanctimonious lechery,

Behind all my petty pleading,
Behind all my hysterical beseeching,
It is all night, with only daylight above it.

Our Father

I was going over to Mummy's place for lunch.
I had said my morning prayers
But I had not expected
My morning prayers materially to alter the day.
Our Father who art in heaven
(Daddy had died two winters ago)
Hallowed be Thy name, Thy kingdom come,
Thy will be done on earth as it is in heaven.

I had decided to catch the number 13 bus to Palmerston Park
From outside Dáil Éireann in Kildare Street
But at the last moment I changed my mind
And I caught the number 14 bus to Dartry.
I do not know why I changed my mind.
Possibly it was because the number 14 came first
Or possibly it was because of the memory
That Daddy, when he was alive, appeared to be perplexed
That I never came home by the number 14 route.
He seemed to think that I should come home by the number
    14 route
And that it was a crime against nature
To come home by the number 13 route.

I sat at the back of the bus on the lower deck
With two bunches of flowers for Mummy in my lap.
When I became aware that the conductor was staring at me
We were stopped outside the National Concert Hall and I
    thought:
Maybe he likes the look of me.
He commented: 'I like your irises.'
'What?'
'Your irises – I like your irises.'

The conductor swayed above me, a knowing smile in his eyes,
As the double-decker lurched around Kelly's Corner –
A landmark of Daddy's
Because on it stood a pub called The Bleeding Horse.
It was the name that attracted him.
He was never inside it in his life.
Every time we drove past The Bleeding Horse
I stared at the blood trickling out of the white mare's withers,
All menstruation and still life.
'I love flowers' – the conductor continued,
Licking the baton of his forefinger –
'My wife says I'm mad and of course I am.
I am mad about flowers.
Lovely irises you have – let me touch them.
I have my own greenhouse – the width of this bus.
My father-in-law built it for me donkey's years ago.
My orchids are in bloom at the moment.
If I'd my way, I'd have nothing but orchids.
All the same a man's got to be pragmatic.'
He clung lithely to the vertical rail as the driver
Flew the bus over Portobello Bridge.

'I've aubergines, peppers, tomatoes, lettuce.
The neighbours are keen on my iceberg lettuce.
They're always pestering me also for my courgettes.
Cucumber too – but you have to be cautious with cucumber.
What with the way the males pollinate the females
You've got to be terribly cautious with your stamens.
Cucumbers are very much that way inclined:
Proliferation, proclivities, you never know where you are.
I have to keep all my cacti on the upper shelves.'

As we slowed down near Rathmines Town Hall, senior
    citizens
On Free Travel called out to the conductor to collect fares.

'Do your duty now, Mister, and collect fares.'
But he waved to the passengers who were disembarking,
A wave that was at once a valediction and a benediction:
'I am not collecting fares this morning,' he confided in me,
'There are times in public transport when it is more
   auspicious
Not to collect fares and today is an auspicious day.
I adore my greenhouse. It can get so hot inside it.
Anything more than a pair of shorts and I'm scalded.'
"Where'd you get your tan?" – the neighbour woman asks me.
"In my greenhouse, where else?" – I answer her back.
A perfect lie.
She wags her finger at my magnolia in the front garden
And she teases me: "Oh, a cherry blossom
Is good enough for the rest of us but not for the likes of you.
For the likes of you it has to be a *magnolium* no less.
Only a *magnolium* is good enough for the likes of you."
That's what she calls it – a *magnolium*.'

We were whizzing past The Pharmacy on Upper Rathmines
   Road
And the Church of Ireland Teacher Training College
But he wanted to dwell on his magnolia:
'It's not a real word at all, you know, "magnolia".
There was a Frenchman – Magnol was his name –
From a place called Montpelier. My wife knew a man
From Montpelier – that's how I remember it.
But I do like your irises.
You have to be patient in this game
And it can be so tedious on top of that.
My grapes, for example. Grapes are too excitable.
I have to keep each grape separate from the other.
Time-consuming it is
Keeping all my grapes separate from each other.
Each grape has to be totally separate from the next grape

183

And only a few weeks ago I lost fifty pounds' worth
Of azaleas – wiped out by Jack Frost.
When I'm skedaddling off to the depot I ask the wife
To remember to open the greenhouse window
But if she remembers to open it,
Sure as not she will forget to close it.
You know what wives are like – not to mention husbands.
At the moment, actually, I'm all Sweet Pea.'
I apologised to him as I dismounted at Dartry.
'Sorry, but I have to get out at this stop.'
'Don't be sorry – be nice to your irises.'

As the bus swerved away from the kerb, I thought:
Amn't I the lucky breadman that I got the Dartry bus
Instead of the Palmerston Park bus,
The number 14 instead of the number 13?
The conductor waved to me as the bus picked up speed.
I looked about me on the street to check if anybody was
     looking.
I blessed myself.
Our Father who art in heaven.
I could feel the conductor's knees brush against my lips
As he ran his fingers through the clay of my hair.

Under the chestnuts and the pine trees and the copper
     beeches
I walk down the street where Daddy slipped on the ice.
He had lain here until a gas worker had found him
And put him in an ambulance and waved goodbye to him,
A gas worker with a piece of piping in his hand.

I press the bell to Mummy's apartment.
I stare up into the surveillance camera lens.
I am a suspect in an interrogation centre,
A forty-five-year-old amoeba dwindling under a microscope.

When a light bulb flashes and her voice crackles over
The intercom I know she can perceive
The panic in the pupils of her son's eyes.
After lunch – soup, a chop, potatoes and peas –
She says that she does not understand my new book of poems
Which are poems I have composed for my dead father.
'But' – she smiles knowingly – 'I like your irises.'

OTHER

BLACKSTAFF PRESS

TITLES BY

PAUL DURCAN

JESUS AND ANGELA

Paul Durcan's reputation as an exciting, highly
original poet has developed rapidly in recent years
with the publication of *The Selected Paul Durcan* (1982),
The Berlin Wall Café (1985; Poetry Book Society
Choice) and *Going Home to Russia* (1987). These three
important titles are published by Blackstaff Press and
are regularly reprinted to keep pace with the demand
generated by Durcan's electrifying poetry readings in
Ireland, Britain, Europe, America and Canada.

Many new fans, keen to read all of Durcan's work,
have been unable to obtain some of his earlier titles.
This book is the author's selection, with revisions,
from work originally published in two separate
books: *Jesus, Break His Fall* (1980) and *Jumping the
Train Tracks with Angela* (1983).

198 × 129 mm; 112 pp; 0 85640 407 1; pb

£5.95

GOING HOME TO RUSSIA

'Paul Durcan's ... collection is, as its title suggests, partly the record of a quest for a spiritual and imaginative home and a celebration of Russia, which the poet visited in 1983 and 1986. Directly and indirectly, the poems on this subject challenge patronising and complacent Western assumptions – both about Russia and the West – and raise questions about the nature of freedom ...

'*Going Home to Russia* is a substantial collection, the work of an inventive and compassionate poet who continues to surprise and provoke and delight.'
Frank Ormsby, BBC Radio Ulster

'Any new work by Paul Durcan is to be hailed. He is a poet of such power, appeal and vitality that publication is to be eagerly anticipated. *Going Home to Russia* is no exception.'
Martin Booth, *Tribune*

198 × 129 mm; 112 pp; 0 85640 386 5; pb
£4.95

ORDERING BLACKSTAFF BOOKS

All Blackstaff Press books are available through bookshops. In the case of difficulty, however, orders can be made directly to the publisher. Indicate clearly the title and number of copies required and send order with your name and address to:

CASH SALES

Blackstaff Press Limited
3 Galway Park
Dundonald
Belfast BT16 0AN
Northern Ireland

Please enclose a remittance to the value of the cover price plus: £1.00 for the first book plus 60p per copy for each additional book ordered to cover postage and packing. Payment should be made in sterling by UK personal cheque, postal order, sterling draft or international money order, made payable to Blackstaff Press Limited.

Applicable only in the UK and Republic of Ireland
Full catalogue available on request